NUMBERS

The Fourth Book of Mo

This WORKBOOK is designed to help assist the diligent study of those who would know the Word of God. It is written in a format that REQUIRES reading of the text from the Authorized King James Version of the Holy Scriptures.

The King James Bible correctly fills all of the available "blanks" in this workbook.

Other workbooks are available by contacting us:

**By FAITH Publications
85 Hendersonville Hwy.
Walterboro, SC 29488**

(843) 538-2269

www.faithbaptistchurch.us

publications@faithbaptistchurch.us

NUMBERS

Numbers 1:1-36:13 (KJV)

And the Lord spake unto Moses in the wilderness of Sinai, _____ the tabernacle of the congregation, on the _____ day of the _____ month, in the _____ year after they were come out of the land of _____ , saying, [2] Take ye the _____ of all the congregation of the children of Israel, after their families, by the house of their fathers, with the number of their names, every _____ by their polls; [3] From _____ years old and upward, all that are _____ to go forth to _____ in Israel: thou and Aaron shall number them by their _____ . [4] And with you there shall be a _____ of every tribe; every one _____ of the _____ of his fathers.

[5] And these are the names of the men that shall stand with you: of the tribe of _____ ; Elizur the son of Shedeur. [6] Of _____ ; Shelumiel the son of Zurishaddai. [7] Of _____ ; Nahshon the son of Amminadab. [8] Of _____ ; Nethaneel the son of Zuar. [9] Of _____ ; Eliab the son of Helon. [10] Of the children of _____ : of _____ ; Elishama the son of Ammihud: of _____ ; Gamaliel the son of Pedahzur. [11] Of _____ ; Abidan the son of Gideoni. [12] Of _____ ; Ahiezer the son of Ammishaddai. [13] Of _____ ; Pagiel the son of Ocran. [14] Of _____ ; Eliasaph the son of Deuel. [15] Of _____ ; Ahira the son of Enan. [16] These were the renowned of the congregation, princes of the tribes of their fathers, heads of thousands in Israel.

[17] And Moses and Aaron took these men which are expressed by their names: [18] And they assembled all the congregation together on the first day of the second month, and they _____ their _____ after their families, by the house of their fathers, according to the number of the names, from twenty years old and upward, by their polls. [19] As the Lord commanded Moses, so he numbered them in the wilderness of Sinai. [20] And the children of Reuben, Israel's _____ son, by their generations, after their families, by the house of their fathers, according to the number of the names, by their polls, every male from twenty years old and upward, all that were able to go forth to war; [21] Those that were numbered of them, even of the tribe of Reuben, were _____ and _____ thousand and _____ hundred.

[22] Of the children of Simeon, by their generations, after their families, by the house of their fathers, those that were numbered of them, according to the number of the names, by their polls, every male from twenty years old and upward, all that were able to go forth to war; [23] Those that were numbered of them, even of the tribe of Simeon, were _____ and _____ thousand and _____ hundred.

[24] Of the children of Gad, by their generations, after their families, by the house of their fathers, according to the number of the names, from twenty years old and upward, all that were able to go forth to war; [25] Those that were numbered of them, even of the tribe of Gad, were _____ and _____ thousand _____ hundred and _____ .

[26] Of the children of Judah, by their generations, after their families, by the house of their fathers, according to the number of the names, from twenty years old and upward, all that were able to go forth to war; [27] Those that were numbered of them, even of the tribe of Judah, were _____ and _____ thousand and _____ hundred.

[28] Of the children of Issachar, by their generations, after their families, by the house of their fathers, according to the number of the names, from twenty years old and upward,

all that were able to go forth to war; [29] Those that were numbered of them, even of the tribe of Issachar, were _____ and _____ thousand and _____ hundred.

[30] Of the children of Zebulun, by their generations, after their families, by the house of their fathers, according to the number of the names, from twenty years old and upward, all that were able to go forth to war; [31] Those that were numbered of them, even of the tribe of Zebulun, were _____ and _____ thousand and _____ hundred.

[32] Of the children of Joseph, namely, of the children of Ephraim, by their generations, after their families, by the house of their fathers, according to the number of the names, from twenty years old and upward, all that were able to go forth to war; [33] Those that were numbered of them, even of the tribe of Ephraim, were _____ thousand and _____ hundred.

[34] Of the children of Manasseh, by their generations, after their families, by the house of their fathers, according to the number of the names, from twenty years old and upward, all that were able to go forth to war; [35] Those that were numbered of them, even of the tribe of Manasseh, were _____ and _____ thousand and _____ hundred.

[36] Of the children of Benjamin, by their generations, after their families, by the house of their fathers, according to the number of the names, from twenty years old and upward, all that were able to go forth to war; [37] Those that were numbered of them, even of the tribe of Benjamin, were _____ and _____ thousand and _____ hundred.

[38] Of the children of Dan, by their generations, after their families, by the house of their fathers, according to the number of the names, from twenty years old and upward, all that were able to go forth to war; [39] Those that were numbered of them, even of the tribe of Dan, were _____ and _____ thousand and _____ hundred.

[40] Of the children of Asher, by their generations, after their families, by the house of their fathers, according to the number of the names, from twenty years old and upward, all that were able to go forth to war; [41] Those that were numbered of them, even of the tribe of Asher, were _____ and _____ thousand and _____ hundred.

[42] Of the children of Naphtali, throughout their generations, after their families, by the house of their fathers, according to the number of the names, from twenty years old and upward, all that were able to go forth to war; [43] Those that were numbered of them, even of the tribe of Naphtali, were _____ and _____ thousand and _____ hundred. [44] These are those that were numbered, which Moses and Aaron numbered, and the princes of Israel, being _____ men: each one was for the house of his fathers. [45] So were all those that were numbered of the children of Israel, by the house of their fathers, from twenty years old and upward, all that were able to go forth to war in Israel; [46] Even all they that were numbered were _____ hundred _____ and _____ thousand and _____ hundred and _____ .

[47] But the _____ after the tribe of their fathers were _____ numbered among them. [48] For the Lord had spoken unto Moses, saying, [49] Only thou shalt not number the tribe of Levi, neither take the sum of them among the children of Israel: [50] But thou shalt _____ the Levites over the _____ of testimony, and over all the _____ thereof, and over all _____ that _____ to it: they shall _____ the tabernacle, and all the vessels thereof; and they shall _____ unto it, and shall _____ round about the tabernacle. [51] And when the tabernacle

setteth forward, the Levites shall take it down: and when the tabernacle is to be pitched, the Levites shall set it up: and the stranger that cometh nigh shall be put to death. [52] And the children of Israel shall pitch their tents, every man by his own camp, and every man by his own _____ , throughout their hosts. [53] But the Levites shall pitch _____ about the tabernacle of testimony, that there be no wrath upon the congregation of the children of Israel: and the Levites shall keep the charge of the tabernacle of testimony. [54] And the children of Israel did according to all that the Lord commanded Moses, so did they.

[2:1] And the Lord spake unto Moses and unto Aaron, saying, [2] Every man of the children of Israel shall pitch by his own standard, with the _____ of their father's house: far off about the tabernacle of the congregation shall they pitch. [3] And on the _____ side toward the rising of the sun shall they of the standard of the camp of _____ pitch throughout their armies: and Nahshon the son of Amminadab shall be captain of the children of Judah. [4] And his host, and those that were numbered of them, were _____ and _____ thousand and _____ hundred. [5] And those that do pitch _____ unto him shall be the tribe of _____ : and Nethaneel the son of Zuar shall be captain of the children of Issachar. [6] And his host, and those that were numbered thereof, were _____ and _____ thousand and _____ hundred. [7] Then the tribe of _____ : and Eliab the son of Helon shall be captain of the children of Zebulun. [8] And his host, and those that were numbered thereof, were _____ and _____ thousand and _____ hundred. [9] All that were numbered in the camp of _____ were an _____ thousand and _____ thousand and _____ thousand and _____ hundred, throughout their armies. These shall _____ set forth.

[10] On the _____ side shall be the standard of the camp of _____ according to their armies: and the captain of the children of Reuben shall be Elizur the son of Shedeur. [11] And his host, and those that were numbered thereof, were _____ and _____ thousand and _____ hundred. [12] And those which pitch by him shall be the tribe of _____ : and the captain of the children of Simeon shall be Shelumiel the son of Zurishaddai. [13] And his host, and those that were numbered of them, were _____ and _____ thousand and _____ hundred. [14] Then the tribe of _____ : and the captain of the sons of Gad shall be Eliasaph the son of Reuel. [15] And his host, and those that were numbered of them, were _____ and _____ thousand and _____ hundred and _____ . [16] All that were numbered in the camp of Reuben were an _____ thousand and _____ and _____ thousand and _____ hundred and _____ , throughout their armies. And they shall set forth in the _____ rank.

[17] Then the tabernacle of the congregation shall set forward with the camp of the _____ in the _____ of the camp: as they encamp, so shall they set forward, every man in his place by their standards.

[18] On the _____ side shall be the standard of the camp of _____ according to their armies: and the captain of the sons of Ephraim shall be Elishama the son of Ammihud. [19] And his host, and those that were numbered of them, were _____ thousand and _____ hundred. [20] And by him shall be the tribe of _____ : and the captain of the children of Manasseh shall be Gamaliel the son of Pedahzur. [21] And his host, and those that were numbered of them, were _____

and _____ thousand and _____ hundred. [22] Then the tribe of _____ : and the captain of the sons of Benjamin shall be Abidan the son of Gideoni. [23] And his host, and those that were numbered of them, were _____ and _____ thousand and _____ hundred. [24] All that were numbered of the camp of Ephraim were an _____ thousand and _____ thousand and an _____ , throughout their armies. And they shall go forward in the _____ rank.

[25] The standard of the camp of _____ shall be on the _____ side by their armies: and the captain of the children of Dan shall be Ahiezer the son of Ammishaddai. [26] And his host, and those that were numbered of them, were _____ and _____ thousand and _____ hundred. [27] And those that encamp by him shall be the tribe of _____ : and the captain of the children of Asher shall be Pagiel the son of Ocran. [28] And his host, and those that were numbered of them, were _____ and _____ thousand and _____ hundred.

[29] Then the tribe of _____ : and the captain of the children of Naphtali shall be Ahira the son of Enan. [30] And his host, and those that were numbered of them, were _____ and _____ thousand and _____ hundred. [31] All they that were numbered in the camp of _____ were an _____ thousand and _____ and _____ thousand and _____ hundred. They shall go _____ with their standards.

[32] These are those which were numbered of the children of Israel by the house of their fathers: all those that were numbered of the camps throughout their hosts were _____ hundred _____ and _____ thousand and _____ hundred and _____ . [33] But the _____ were _____ numbered among the children of Israel; as the Lord commanded Moses. [34] And the children of Israel did according to all that the Lord commanded Moses: so they _____ by their _____ , and so they set _____ , every one after their _____ , according to the house of their fathers.

[3:1] These also are the generations of _____ and _____ in the day that the Lord spake with Moses in mount Sinai. [2] And these are the names of the _____ of Aaron; _____ the firstborn, and _____ , _____ , and _____ . [3] These are the names of the sons of Aaron, the _____ which were _____ , whom he _____ to _____ in the priest's office. [4] And Nadab and Abihu _____ before the Lord, when they _____ strange _____ before the Lord, in the wilderness of Sinai, and they had _____ children: and _____ and _____ ministered in the priest's office in the _____ of Aaron their father.

[5] And the Lord spake unto Moses, saying, [6] Bring the tribe of _____ near, and present them before Aaron the priest, that they may _____ unto _____ . [7] And they shall _____ his _____ , and the charge of the whole congregation before the tabernacle of the congregation, to _____ the _____ of the tabernacle. [8] And they shall keep all the _____ of the tabernacle of the congregation, and the charge of the children of Israel, to do the service of the tabernacle. [9] And thou shalt _____ the _____ unto Aaron and to his sons: they are wholly given unto him out of the children of Israel. [10] And thou shalt appoint Aaron and his sons, and they shall _____ on their priest's office: and the stranger that cometh nigh shall be put to death. [11] And the Lord spake unto Moses, saying, [12] And I, behold, I have taken the Levites from among the children of Israel instead of all the

firstborn that openeth the matrix among the children of Israel: therefore the Levites shall be mine; [13] Because all the firstborn are mine; for on the day that I smote all the firstborn in the land of Egypt I hallowed unto me all the firstborn in Israel, both man and beast: mine shall they be: I am the Lord.

[14] And the Lord spake unto Moses in the wilderness of Sinai, saying, [15] _____ the children of _____ after the house of their fathers, by their families: every male from a _____ old and upward shalt thou number them. [16] And Moses numbered them according to the word of the Lord, as he was commanded. [17] And these were the sons of Levi by their names; _____ , and _____ , and _____ . [18] And these are the names of the sons of _____ by their families; Libni, and Shimei. [19] And the sons of _____ by their families; Amram, and Izehar, Hebron, and Uzziel. [20] And the sons of _____ by their families; Mahli, and Mushi. These are the families of the Levites according to the house of their fathers. [21] Of _____ was the family of the Libnites, and the family of the Shimites: these are the families of the _____ . [22] Those that were numbered of them, according to the number of all the males, from a month old and upward, even those that were numbered of them were _____ thousand and _____ hundred. [23] The families of the _____ shall pitch _____ the tabernacle _____ . [24] And the chief of the house of the father of the Gershonites shall be Eliasaph the son of Lael. [25] And the charge of the sons of Gershon in the tabernacle of the congregation shall be the _____ , and the _____ , the _____ thereof, and the _____ for the _____ of the tabernacle of the congregation, [26] And the hangings of the _____ , and the _____ for the door of the court, which is by the tabernacle, and by the _____ round about, and the _____ of it for all the service thereof.

[27] And of _____ was the family of the Amramites, and the family of the Izeharites, and the family of the Hebronites, and the family of the Uzzielites: these are the families of the _____ . [28] In the number of all the males, from a month old and upward, were _____ thousand and _____ hundred, keeping the _____ of the _____ . [29] The families of the sons of Kohath shall pitch on the _____ of the tabernacle _____ . [30] And the chief of the house of the father of the families of the Kohathites shall be Elizaphan the son of Uzziel. [31] And their charge shall be the _____ , and the _____ , and the _____ , and the _____ , and the _____ of the sanctuary wherewith they minister, and the _____ , and all the _____ thereof. [32] And _____ the son of Aaron the priest shall be _____ over the _____ of the _____ , and have the _____ of them that keep the charge of the sanctuary.

[33] Of _____ was the family of the Mahlites, and the family of the Mushites: these are the families of Merari. [34] And those that were numbered of them, according to the number of all the males, from a month old and upward, were _____ thousand and _____ hundred. [35] And the chief of the house of the father of the families of Merari was Zuriel the son of Abihail: these shall pitch on the _____ of the tabernacle _____ . [36] And under the custody and charge of the sons of Merari shall be the _____ of the tabernacle, and the _____ thereof, and the _____ thereof, and the _____ thereof, and all the _____ thereof, and all that _____ thereto, [37] And the _____ of the court round about, and their _____ , and their _____ , and their _____ .

[38] But those that encamp _____ the tabernacle toward the _____ , even before the tabernacle of the congregation eastward, shall be _____ , and _____ and his _____ , keeping the _____ of the _____ for the _____ of the children of _____ ; and the stranger that cometh nigh shall be put to death. [39] All that were numbered of the _____ , which Moses and Aaron numbered at the commandment of the Lord, throughout their families, all the males from a month old and upward, were _____ and _____ thousand.

[40] And the Lord said unto Moses, _____ all the _____ of the males of the children of Israel from a month old and upward, and take the number of their names. [41] And thou shalt take the Levites for me (I am the Lord) instead of all the firstborn among the children of Israel; and the cattle of the Levites instead of all the firstlings among the cattle of the children of Israel. [42] And Moses numbered, as the Lord commanded him, all the firstborn among the children of Israel. [43] And all the firstborn males by the number of names, from a month old and upward, of those that were numbered of them, were _____ and _____ thousand _____ hundred and _____ and _____ .

[44] And the Lord spake unto Moses, saying, [45] Take the Levites instead of all the firstborn among the children of Israel, and the _____ of the Levites instead of their cattle; and the Levites shall be mine: I am the Lord. [46] And for those that are to be redeemed of the two hundred and threescore and thirteen of the firstborn of the children of Israel, which are more than the Levites; [47] Thou shalt even take _____ shekels _____ by the poll, after the shekel of the sanctuary shalt thou take them: (the shekel is twenty gerahs:) [48] And thou shalt _____ the _____ , wherewith the odd number of them is to be redeemed, unto _____ and to his _____ . [49] And Moses took the redemption money of them that were over and above them that were redeemed by the Levites: [50] Of the firstborn of the children of Israel took he the money; a thousand three hundred and threescore and five shekels, after the shekel of the sanctuary: [51] And Moses gave the money of them that were redeemed unto Aaron and to his sons, according to the word of the Lord, as the Lord commanded Moses.

[4:1] And the Lord spake unto Moses and unto Aaron, saying, [2] Take the sum of the sons of Kohath from among the sons of Levi, after their families, by the house of their fathers, [3] From _____ years old and upward even until _____ years old, all that enter into the host, to do the _____ in the _____ of the congregation. [4] This shall be the service of the sons of Kohath in the tabernacle of the congregation, about the _____ holy things:

[5] And when the camp setteth forward, _____ shall come, and his _____ , and they shall take down the _____ vail, and cover the _____ of testimony with it: [6] And shall put thereon the covering of badgers' skins, and shall spread over it a cloth wholly of _____ , and shall put in the staves thereof. [7] And upon the table of _____ they shall spread a cloth of _____ , and put thereon the dishes, and the spoons, and the bowls, and covers to cover withal: and the continual bread shall be thereon: [8] And they shall spread upon them a cloth of _____ , and cover the same with a covering of badgers' skins, and shall put in the staves thereof. [9] And they shall take a cloth of _____ , and cover the candlestick of the light, and his lamps, and his tongs, and his snuffdishes, and all the _____ vessels thereof, wherewith they minister unto it: [10] And they shall put it and all the vessels thereof within a covering of

badgers' skins, and shall put it upon a bar. [11] And upon the golden altar they shall spread a cloth of _____, and cover it with a covering of badgers' skins, and shall put to the staves thereof: [12] And they shall take all the instruments of _____, wherewith they minister in the sanctuary, and put them in a cloth of _____, and cover them with a covering of badgers' skins, and shall put them on a bar: [13] And they shall take away the ashes from the altar, and spread a purple cloth thereon: [14] And they shall put upon it all the vessels thereof, wherewith they minister about it, even the censers, the fleshhooks, and the shovels, and the basons, all the vessels of the altar; and they shall spread upon it a covering of badgers' skins, and put to the staves of it. [15] And when Aaron and his sons have made an end of covering the sanctuary, and all the vessels of the sanctuary, as the camp is to set forward; after that, the sons of Kohath shall come to _____ it: but they shall not _____ any holy thing, lest they _____. These things are the burden of the sons of Kohath in the tabernacle of the congregation.

[16] And to the office of Eleazar the son of Aaron the priest pertaineth the _____ for the light, and the sweet incense, and the daily meat offering, and the anointing _____, and the _____ of all the tabernacle, and of all that therein is, in the sanctuary, and in the vessels thereof.

[17] And the Lord spake unto Moses and unto Aaron, saying, [18] Cut ye not off the tribe of the families of the Kohathites from among the Levites: [19] But thus do unto them, that they may live, and not die, when they approach unto the most _____ things: Aaron and his sons shall go in, and appoint them every one to his service and to his burden: [20] But they shall not go in to _____ when the holy things are _____, lest they die.

[21] And the Lord spake unto Moses, saying, [22] Take also the sum of the sons of _____, throughout the houses of their fathers, by their families; [23] From _____ years old and upward until _____ years old shalt thou number them; all that enter in to perform the service, to do the _____ in the tabernacle of the congregation. [24] This is the service of the families of the Gershonites, to _____, and for burdens: [25] And they shall bear the curtains of the tabernacle, and the tabernacle of the congregation, his covering, and the covering of the badgers' skins that is above upon it, and the hanging for the door of the tabernacle of the congregation, [26] And the hangings of the court, and the hanging for the door of the gate of the court, which is by the tabernacle and by the altar round about, and their cords, and all the instruments of their service, and all that is made for them: so shall they _____.
[27] At the appointment of Aaron and his sons shall be all the service of the sons of the Gershonites, in all their burdens, and in all their service: and ye shall appoint unto them in charge all their burdens. [28] This is the _____ of the families of the sons of Gershon in the tabernacle of the congregation: and their charge shall be under the hand of Ithamar the son of Aaron the priest.

[29] As for the sons of _____, thou shalt number them after their families, by the house of their fathers; [30] From _____ years old and upward even unto _____ years old shalt thou number them, every one that entereth into the _____, to do the _____ of the tabernacle of the congregation. [31] And this is the charge of their burden, according to all their service in the tabernacle of the congregation; the boards of the tabernacle, and the bars thereof, and the pillars thereof, and sockets thereof, [32] And the pillars of the court round about, and their sockets, and

their pins, and their cords, with all their instruments, and with all their service: and by _____ ye shall reckon the instruments of the charge of their burden. [33] This is the service of the families of the sons of _____ , according to all their service, in the tabernacle of the congregation, under the hand of Ithamar the son of Aaron the priest.

[34] And Moses and Aaron and the chief of the congregation numbered the sons of the Kohathites after their families, and after the house of their fathers, [35] From thirty years old and upward even unto fifty years old, every one that entereth into the service, for the work in the tabernacle of the congregation: [36] And those that were numbered of them by their families were _____ thousand _____ hundred and _____ . [37] These were they that were numbered of the families of the _____ , all that might do _____ _____ the tabernacle of the congregation, which Moses and Aaron did number according to the commandment of the Lord by the hand of Moses. [38] And those that were numbered of the sons of _____ , throughout their families, and by the house of their fathers, [39] From thirty years old and upward even unto fifty years old, every one that entereth into the _____ , _____ the work in the tabernacle of the congregation, [40] Even those that were numbered of them, throughout their families, by the house of their fathers, were _____ thousand and _____ hundred and _____ . [41] These are they that were numbered of the families of the sons of Gershon, of all that might do service in the tabernacle of the congregation, whom Moses and Aaron did number according to the commandment of the Lord.

[42] And those that were numbered of the families of the sons of _____ , throughout their families, by the house of their fathers, [43] From thirty years old and upward even unto fifty years old, every one that entereth into the service, for the _____ in the tabernacle of the congregation, [44] Even those that were numbered of them after their families, were _____ thousand and _____ hundred. [45] These be those that were numbered of the families of the sons of Merari, whom Moses and Aaron numbered according to the word of the Lord by the hand of Moses. [46] All those that were numbered of the Levites, whom Moses and Aaron and the chief of Israel numbered, after their families, and after the house of their fathers, [47] From thirty years old and upward even unto fifty years old, every one that came to _____ the _____ of the ministry, and the _____ of the _____ in the tabernacle of the congregation, [48] Even those that were numbered of them, were _____ thousand and _____ hundred and fourscore. [49] According to the commandment of the Lord they were numbered by the hand of Moses, every one according to his service, and according to his burden: thus were they numbered of him, as the Lord commanded Moses.

[5:1] And the Lord spake unto Moses, saying, [2] _____ the children of Israel, that they put out of the camp every _____ , and every one that hath an _____ , and whosoever is _____ by the dead: [3] Both male and female shall ye put _____ , without the camp shall ye put them; that they defile _____ their camps, in the midst whereof I dwell. [4] And the children of Israel did so, and put them out without the camp: as the Lord spake unto Moses, so did the children of Israel.

[5] And the Lord spake unto Moses, saying, [6] Speak unto the children of Israel, When a man or woman shall commit any _____ that men commit, to do a _____ against the Lord, and that person be _____ ; [7] Then they shall _____ their sin which they have done: and he shall _____ his trespass with

the _____ thereof, and _____ unto it the _____ part thereof, and give it unto him against whom he hath trespassed. [8] But if the man have no kinsman to recompense the trespass unto, let the trespass be _____ unto the _____ , even to the _____ ; beside the ram of the atonement, whereby an atonement shall be made for him. [9] And every offering of all the holy things of the children of Israel, which they bring unto the _____ , shall be _____ . [10] And every man's hallowed things shall be his: whatsoever any man giveth the _____ , it shall be

_____ .

   [11] And the Lord spake unto Moses, saying, [12] Speak unto the children of Israel, and say unto them, If any man's _____ go aside, and commit a _____ against him, [13] And a man _____ with her _____ , and it be hid from the eyes of her husband, and be kept close, and she be defiled, and there be no witness against her, neither she be taken with the manner; [14] And the _____ of _____ come upon him, and he be jealous of his wife, and she be _____ : or if the spirit of jealousy come upon him, and he be jealous of his wife, and she be _____ defiled: [15] Then shall the man bring his wife unto the priest, and he shall bring her _____ for her, the tenth part of an ephah of barley meal; he shall pour no _____ upon it, nor put frankincense thereon; for it is an offering of _____ , an offering of memorial, bringing _____ to remembrance. [16] And the priest shall bring her near, and set her before the Lord: [17] And the priest shall take holy water in an earthen vessel; and of the dust that is in the floor of the tabernacle the priest shall take, and put it into the water: [18] And the priest shall set the woman before the Lord, and uncover the woman's head, and put the offering of memorial in her hands, which is the jealousy offering: and the priest shall have in his hand the bitter water that causeth the

_____ : [19] And the priest shall charge her by an _____ , and say unto the woman, If no man have lain with thee, and if thou hast not gone aside to uncleanness with another instead of thy husband, be thou _____ from this bitter water that causeth the curse: [20] But if thou hast gone aside to another instead of thy husband, and if thou be defiled, and some man have lain with thee beside thine husband: [21] Then the priest shall charge the woman with an oath of _____ , and the priest shall say unto the woman, The Lord make thee a _____ and an oath among thy people, when the Lord doth make thy thigh to _____ , and thy _____ to swell; [22] And this water that causeth the curse shall go into thy bowels, to make thy belly to swell, and thy thigh to rot: And the woman shall say, _____ , _____ . [23] And the priest shall write these curses in a book, and he shall blot them out with the bitter water: [24] And he shall cause the woman to drink the bitter water that causeth the curse: and the water that causeth the curse shall enter into her, and become bitter. [25] Then the priest shall take the jealousy offering out of the woman's hand, and shall wave the offering before the Lord, and offer it upon the altar: [26] And the priest shall take an handful of the offering, even the memorial thereof, and burn it upon the altar, and afterward shall cause the woman to drink the water. [27] And when he hath made her to drink the water, then it shall come to pass, that, if she be defiled, and have done trespass against her husband, that the water that causeth the curse shall enter into her, and become bitter, and her belly shall swell, and her thigh shall rot: and the woman shall be a curse among her people. [28] And if the woman be not defiled, but be clean; then she shall be _____ , and shall _____ seed. [29] This is the law of _____ , when a wife goeth aside to another instead of her husband, and is defiled; [30] _____ when the spirit of jealousy cometh upon him, and he be jealous over his wife, and shall set the woman before the Lord, and the priest shall execute upon her all this law. [31] Then shall the man be guiltless from iniquity, and this woman shall bear her iniquity.

[6:1] And the Lord spake unto Moses, saying, [2] Speak unto the children of Israel, and say unto them, When either _____ or _____ shall _____ themselves to _____ a vow of a _____ , to separate themselves unto the Lord: [3] He shall separate himself from _____ and _____ drink, and shall drink no _____ of _____ , or _____ of _____ drink, neither shall he drink any _____ of _____ , nor eat _____ grapes, or _____ . [4] _____ the days of his _____ shall he eat _____ that is made of the _____ tree, from the _____ even to the _____ . [5] All the days of the vow of his separation there shall no _____ come upon his head: until the days be fulfilled, in the which he separateth himself unto the _____ , he shall be _____ , and shall let the locks of the hair of his head grow. [6] All the days that he separateth himself unto the Lord he shall come at no _____ body. [7] He shall not make himself _____ for his father, or for his mother, for his brother, or for his sister, when they _____ : because the _____ of his God is upon his head. [8] _____ the _____ of his _____ he is _____ unto the Lord. [9] And if any man die very suddenly by him, and he hath defiled the head of his consecration; then he shall shave his head in the day of his cleansing, on the seventh day shall he shave it. [10] And on the eighth day he shall bring two turtles, or two young pigeons, to the priest, to the door of the tabernacle of the congregation: [11] And the priest shall offer the one for a sin offering, and the other for a burnt offering, and make an _____ for him, for that he sinned by the dead, and shall hallow his head that same day. [12] And he shall consecrate unto the Lord the days of his separation, and shall bring a lamb of the first year for a trespass offering: but the days that were before shall be lost, because his _____ was defiled.

[13] And this is the law of the _____ , when the days of his separation are _____ : he shall be brought unto the door of the tabernacle of the congregation: [14] And he shall offer his offering unto the Lord, one he lamb of the first year without blemish for a burnt offering, and one ewe lamb of the first year without blemish for a sin offering, and one ram without blemish for peace offerings, [15] And a basket of unleavened bread, cakes of fine flour mingled with _____ , and wafers of unleavened bread anointed with _____ , and their meat offering, and their drink offerings. [16] And the priest shall bring them before the Lord, and shall offer his sin offering, and his burnt offering: [17] And he shall offer the ram for a sacrifice of peace offerings unto the Lord, with the basket of unleavened bread: the priest shall offer also his meat offering, and his drink offering. [18] And the _____ shall _____ the head of his separation at the door of the tabernacle of the congregation, and shall take the _____ of the head of his separation, and put it in the _____ which is under the sacrifice of the peace offerings. [19] And the priest shall take the sodden shoulder of the ram, and one unleavened cake out of the basket, and one unleavened wafer, and shall put them upon the _____ of the Nazarite, after the hair of his separation is shaven: [20] And the priest shall wave them for a wave offering before the Lord: this is _____ for the priest, with the wave breast and heave shoulder: and after that the

Nazarite may drink wine. [21] This is the _____ of the _____ who hath _____ , and of his offering unto the Lord for his separation, beside that that his hand shall get: according to the vow which he vowed, so he must do after the law of his separation.

[22] And the Lord spake unto Moses, saying, [23] Speak unto Aaron and unto his sons, saying, On this wise ye shall _____ the children of Israel, saying unto them, [24] The Lord _____ thee, and _____ thee: [25] The Lord make his face _____ upon thee, and be _____ unto thee: [26] The Lord _____ up his _____ upon thee, and give thee _____ . [27] And they shall put my _____ upon the children of Israel; and I will _____ them.

[7:1] And it came to pass on the day that Moses had fully set up the tabernacle, and had anointed it, and sanctified it, and all the instruments thereof, both the altar and all the vessels thereof, and had anointed them, and sanctified them; [2] That the princes of Israel, heads of the house of their fathers, who were the princes of the tribes, and were over them that were numbered, offered: [3] And they brought their _____ before the Lord, six covered wagons, and twelve oxen; a wagon for two of the princes, and for each one an ox: and they brought them before the tabernacle. [4] And the Lord spake unto Moses, saying, [5] _____ it of them, that they may be to _____ the _____ of the tabernacle of the congregation; and thou shalt _____ them unto the _____ , to every man _____ to his _____ . [6] And Moses took the wagons and the oxen, and gave them unto the Levites. [7] Two wagons and four oxen he gave unto the sons of _____ , according to their service: [8] And four wagons and eight oxen he gave unto the sons of _____ , according unto their service, under the hand of Ithamar the son of Aaron the priest. [9] But unto the sons of _____ he gave _____ : because the service of the sanctuary belonging unto them was that they should _____ upon their _____ .

[10] And the princes offered for _____ of the altar in the day that it was anointed, even the princes offered their offering before the altar. [11] And the Lord said unto Moses, They shall offer their offering, each prince on his day, for the dedicating of the altar.

[12] And he that offered his offering the first day was Nahshon the son of Amminadab, of the tribe of _____ : [13] And his offering was one silver _____ , the weight thereof was an hundred and thirty shekels, one silver bowl of seventy shekels, after the shekel of the sanctuary; both of them were full of fine flour mingled with _____ for a meat offering: [14] One spoon of ten shekels of gold, full of incense: [15] One young bullock, one ram, one lamb of the first year, for a burnt offering: [16] One kid of the goats for a sin offering: [17] And for a sacrifice of peace offerings, two oxen, five rams, five he goats, five lambs of the first year: this was the offering of Nahshon the son of Amminadab.

[18] On the second day Nethaneel the son of Zuar, prince of _____ , did offer: [19] He offered for his offering one silver charger, the weight whereof was an hundred and thirty shekels, one silver _____ of seventy shekels, after the shekel of the sanctuary; both of them full of fine flour mingled with _____ for a meat offering: [20] One spoon of gold of ten shekels, full of incense: [21] One young bullock, one ram, one lamb of the first year, for a burnt offering: [22] One kid of the goats for a sin

offering: [23] And for a sacrifice of peace offerings, two oxen, five rams, five he goats, five lambs of the first year: this was the offering of Nethaneel the son of Zuar.

[24] On the third day Eliab the son of Helon, prince of the children of _____ , did offer: [25] His offering was one silver charger, the weight whereof was an hundred and thirty shekels, one silver bowl of seventy shekels, after the shekel of the sanctuary; both of them full of fine _____ mingled with _____ for a meat offering: [26] One golden spoon of ten shekels, full of incense: [27] One young bullock, one ram, one lamb of the first year, for a burnt offering: [28] One kid of the goats for a sin offering: [29] And for a sacrifice of peace offerings, two oxen, five rams, five he goats, five lambs of the first year: this was the offering of Eliab the son of Helon.

[30] On the fourth day Elizur the son of Shedeur, prince of the children of _____ , did offer: [31] His offering was one silver charger of the weight of an hundred and thirty shekels, one silver bowl of seventy shekels, after the shekel of the sanctuary; both of them full of fine flour mingled with _____ for a meat offering: [32] One golden _____ of ten shekels, full of incense: [33] One young bullock, one ram, one lamb of the first year, for a burnt offering: [34] One kid of the goats for a sin offering: [35] And for a sacrifice of peace offerings, two oxen, five rams, five he goats, five lambs of the first year: this was the offering of Elizur the son of Shedeur.

[36] On the fifth day Shelumiel the son of Zurishaddai, prince of the children of _____ , did offer: [37] His offering was one silver charger, the weight whereof was an hundred and thirty shekels, one silver bowl of seventy shekels, after the shekel of the sanctuary; both of them full of fine flour mingled with _____ for a meat offering: [38] One golden spoon of ten shekels, full of _____ : [39] One young bullock, one ram, one lamb of the first year, for a burnt offering: [40] One kid of the goats for a sin offering: [41] And for a sacrifice of peace offerings, two oxen, five rams, five he goats, five lambs of the first year: this was the offering of Shelumiel the son of Zurishaddai.

[42] On the sixth day Eliasaph the son of Deuel, prince of the children of _____ , offered: [43] His offering was one silver charger of the weight of an hundred and thirty shekels, a silver bowl of seventy shekels, after the shekel of the sanctuary; both of them full of fine flour mingled with _____ for a meat offering: [44] One golden spoon of ten shekels, full of incense: [45] One young _____ , one ram, one lamb of the first year, for a burnt offering: [46] One kid of the goats for a sin offering: [47] And for a sacrifice of peace offerings, two oxen, five rams, five he goats, five lambs of the first year: this was the offering of Eliasaph the son of Deuel.

[48] On the seventh day Elishama the son of Ammihud, prince of the children of _____ , offered: [49] His offering was one silver charger, the weight whereof was an hundred and thirty shekels, one silver bowl of seventy shekels, after the shekel of the sanctuary; both of them full of fine flour mingled with _____ for a meat offering: [50] One golden spoon of ten shekels, full of incense: [51] One young bullock, one _____ , one lamb of the first year, for a burnt offering: [52] one kid of the goats for a sin offering: [53] And for a sacrifice of peace offerings, two oxen, five rams, five he goats, five lambs of the first year: this was the offering of Elishama the son of Ammihud.

[54] On the eighth day offered Gamaliel the son of Pedahzur, prince of the children of _____ : [55] His offering was one silver charger of the weight of an hundred and thirty shekels, one silver bowl of seventy shekels, after the shekel of the sanctuary; both of them full of fine flour mingled with _____ for a meat offering: [56] One golden

spoon of ten shekels, full of incense: [57] One young bullock, one ram, one _____ of the first year, for a burnt offering: [58] One kid of the goats for a sin offering: [59] And for a sacrifice of peace offerings, two oxen, five rams, five he goats, five lambs of the first year: this was the offering of Gamaliel the son of Pedahzur.

[60] On the ninth day Abidan the son of Gideoni, prince of the children of _____ , offered: [61] His offering was one silver charger, the weight whereof was an hundred and thirty shekels, one silver bowl of seventy shekels, after the shekel of the sanctuary; both of them full of fine flour mingled with _____ for a meat offering: [62] One golden spoon of ten shekels, full of incense: [63] One young bullock, one ram, one lamb of the first year, for a _____ offering: [64] One kid of the goats for a sin offering: [65] And for a sacrifice of peace offerings, two oxen, five rams, five he goats, five lambs of the first year: this was the offering of Abidan the son of Gideoni.

[66] On the tenth day Ahiezer the son of Ammishaddai, prince of the children of _____ , offered: [67] His offering was one silver charger, the weight whereof was an hundred and thirty shekels, one silver bowl of seventy shekels, after the shekel of the sanctuary; both of them full of fine flour mingled with _____ for a meat offering: [68] One golden spoon of ten shekels, full of incense: [69] One young bullock, one ram, one lamb of the first year, for a burnt offering: [70] One _____ of the goats for a sin offering: [71] And for a sacrifice of peace offerings, two oxen, five rams, five he goats, five lambs of the first year: this was the offering of Ahiezer the son of Ammishaddai.

[72] On the eleventh day Pagiel the son of Ocran, prince of the children of _____ , offered: [73] His offering was one silver charger, the weight whereof was an hundred and thirty shekels, one silver bowl of seventy shekels, after the shekel of the sanctuary; both of them full of fine flour mingled with _____ for a meat offering: [74] One golden spoon of ten shekels, full of incense: [75] One young bullock, one ram, one lamb of the first year, for a burnt offering: [76] One kid of the goats for a _____ offering: [77] And for a sacrifice of peace offerings, two oxen, five rams, five he goats, five lambs of the first year: this was the offering of Pagiel the son of Ocran.

[78] On the twelfth day Ahira the son of Enan, prince of the children of _____ , offered: [79] His offering was one silver charger, the weight whereof was an hundred and thirty shekels, one silver bowl of seventy shekels, after the shekel of the sanctuary; both of them full of fine flour mingled with _____ for a meat offering: [80] One golden spoon of ten shekels, full of incense: [81] One young bullock, one ram, one lamb of the first year, for a burnt offering: [82] One kid of the goats for a sin offering: [83] And for a sacrifice of _____ offerings, two oxen, five rams, five he goats, five lambs of the first year: this was the offering of Ahira the son of Enan. [84] This was the dedication of the altar, in the day when it was anointed, by the princes of Israel: twelve chargers of silver, twelve silver bowls, twelve spoons of gold: [85] Each charger of silver weighing an hundred and thirty shekels, each bowl seventy: all the silver vessels weighed two thousand and four hundred shekels, after the shekel of the sanctuary: [86] The golden spoons were twelve, full of incense, weighing ten shekels apiece, after the shekel of the sanctuary: all the gold of the spoons was an hundred and twenty shekels. [87] All the oxen for the burnt offering were twelve bullocks, the rams twelve, the lambs of the first year twelve, with their meat offering: and the kids of the goats for sin offering twelve. [88] And all the oxen for the sacrifice of the peace offerings were twenty and four

bullocks, the rams sixty, the he goats sixty, the lambs of the first year sixty. This was the dedication of the altar, after that it was anointed. [89] And when Moses was gone into the tabernacle of the congregation to speak with him, then he heard the _____ of one speaking unto him from off the _____ seat that was upon the _____ of testimony, from _____ the two _____ : and he _____ unto him.

[8:1] And the Lord spake unto Moses, saying, [2] Speak unto Aaron, and say unto him, When thou _____ the _____ , the seven lamps shall give light over against the candlestick. [3] And Aaron did so; he lighted the lamps thereof over against the candlestick, as the Lord commanded Moses. [4] And this work of the candlestick was of beaten gold, unto the shaft thereof, unto the flowers thereof, was beaten work: according unto the pattern which the Lord had shewed Moses, so he made the candlestick.

[5] And the Lord spake unto Moses, saying, [6] Take the Levites from among the children of Israel, and cleanse them. [7] And thus shalt thou do unto them, to cleanse them: Sprinkle water of purifying upon them, and let them shave all their flesh, and let them wash their clothes, and so make themselves clean. [8] Then let them take a young bullock with his meat offering, even fine flour mingled with _____ , and another young bullock shalt thou take for a sin offering. [9] And thou shalt bring the Levites before the tabernacle of the congregation: and thou shalt gather the whole assembly of the children of Israel together: [10] And thou shalt bring the Levites before the Lord: and the children of Israel shall put their _____ upon the Levites: [11] And Aaron shall offer the Levites before the Lord for an offering of the children of Israel, that they may execute the service of the Lord. [12] And the Levites shall lay their hands upon the heads of the bullocks: and thou shalt offer the one for a sin offering, and the other for a burnt offering, unto the Lord, to make an _____ for the Levites. [13] And thou shalt set the Levites before Aaron, and before his sons, and offer them for an offering unto the Lord. [14] Thus shalt thou separate the Levites from among the children of Israel: and the Levites shall be mine. [15] And after that shall the Levites go in to do the service of the tabernacle of the congregation: and thou shalt cleanse them, and offer them for an offering. [16] For they are wholly given unto me from among the children of Israel; instead of such as open every womb, even instead of the firstborn of all the children of Israel, have I taken them unto me. [17] For all the firstborn of the children of Israel are mine, both man and beast: on the day that I smote every firstborn in the land of Egypt I sanctified them for myself. [18] And I have taken the Levites for all the firstborn of the children of Israel. [19] And I have given the _____ as a _____ to _____ and to his sons from among the children of Israel, to do the service of the children of Israel in the tabernacle of the congregation, and to make an atonement for the children of Israel: that there be no plague among the children of Israel, when the children of Israel come nigh unto the sanctuary. [20] And Moses, and Aaron, and all the congregation of the children of Israel, did to the Levites according unto all that the Lord commanded Moses concerning the Levites, so did the children of Israel unto them. [21] And the Levites were purified, and they washed their clothes; and Aaron offered them as an offering before the Lord; and Aaron made an atonement for them to cleanse them. [22] And after that went the Levites in to do their service in the tabernacle of the congregation before Aaron, and before his sons: as the Lord had commanded Moses concerning the Levites, so did they unto them.

NUMBERS

[23] And the Lord spake unto Moses, saying, [24] This is it that belongeth unto the Levites: from _____ and _____ years old and upward they shall go in to _____ upon the _____ of the tabernacle of the congregation: [25] And from the age of _____ years they shall _____ waiting upon the service thereof, and shall serve no more: [26] But shall _____ with their _____ in the _____ of the congregation, to keep the charge, and shall do no service. Thus shalt thou do unto the Levites touching their charge.

[9:1] And the Lord spake unto Moses in the wilderness of Sinai, in the first month of the second year after they were come out of the land of Egypt, saying, [2] Let the children of Israel also keep the _____ at his appointed season. [3] In the _____ day of this month, at even, ye shall keep it in his appointed season: according to all the rites of it, and according to all the ceremonies thereof, shall ye keep it. [4] And Moses spake unto the children of Israel, that they should keep the passover. [5] And they kept the passover on the fourteenth day of the first month at even in the wilderness of Sinai: according to all that the Lord commanded Moses, so did the children of Israel.

[6] And there were certain men, who were defiled by the dead body of a man, that they could _____ keep the _____ on _____ day: and they came before Moses and before Aaron on that day: [7] And those men said unto him, We are defiled by the dead body of a man: wherefore are we kept back, that we may not offer an offering of the Lord in his appointed season among the children of Israel? [8] And Moses said unto them, Stand still, and I will hear what the Lord will command concerning you.

[9] And the Lord spake unto Moses, saying, [10] Speak unto the children of Israel, saying, If any man of you or of your posterity shall be unclean by reason of a dead body, or be in a journey afar off, yet he shall keep the passover unto the Lord. [11] The _____ day of the _____ month at even they shall keep it, and eat it with unleavened bread and bitter herbs. [12] They shall leave none of it unto the morning, nor break any bone of it: according to all the ordinances of the passover they shall keep it. [13] But the man that is clean, and is not in a journey, and forbeareth to keep the passover, even the same soul shall be cut off from among his people: because he brought not the offering of the Lord in his appointed season, that man shall bear his sin. [14] And if a stranger shall sojourn among you, and will keep the passover unto the Lord; according to the ordinance of the passover, and according to the manner thereof, so shall he do: ye shall have one ordinance, both for the stranger, and for him that was born in the land.

[15] And on the day that the tabernacle was reared up the _____ covered the tabernacle, namely, the tent of the _____ : and at even there was upon the tabernacle as it were the appearance of _____ , until the morning. [16] So it was alway: the _____ covered it by _____ , and the appearance of _____ by _____ . [17] And when the cloud was _____ up from the tabernacle, then after that the children of Israel _____ : and in the place where the cloud _____ , there the children of Israel _____ their tents. [18] At the _____ of the Lord the children of Israel _____ , and at the _____ of the Lord they _____ : as long as the cloud abode upon the tabernacle they _____ in their tents. [19] And when the cloud _____ long upon the tabernacle many days, then the children of Israel kept the charge of the Lord, and journeyed _____ . [20] And so it

was, when the cloud was a few days upon the tabernacle; according to the commandment of the Lord they abode in their tents, and according to the commandment of the Lord they journeyed. [21] And so it was, when the cloud abode from even unto the morning, and that the cloud was taken up in the morning, then they journeyed: whether it was by _____ or by _____ that the cloud was taken up, they _____ . [22] Or whether it were two days, or a month, or a year, that the cloud tarried upon the tabernacle, remaining thereon, the children of Israel abode in their tents, and journeyed not: but when it was taken up, they journeyed. [23] At the commandment of the Lord they rested in the tents, and at the commandment of the Lord they journeyed: they kept the charge of the Lord, at the commandment of the Lord by the hand of Moses.

[10:1] And the Lord spake unto Moses, saying, [2] Make thee two _____ of silver; of a whole piece shalt thou make them: that thou mayest use them for the _____ of the assembly, and for the journeying of the camps. [3] And when they shall blow with them, all the assembly shall _____ themselves to thee at the door of the tabernacle of the congregation. [4] And if they blow but with _____ trumpet, then the _____ , which are heads of the thousands of Israel, shall gather themselves unto thee. [5] When ye blow an _____ , then the camps that lie on the _____ parts shall go _____ . [6] When ye blow an alarm the _____ time, then the camps that lie on the _____ side shall take their journey: they shall blow an alarm for their journeys. [7] But when the congregation is to be gathered together, ye shall blow, but ye shall not sound an alarm. [8] And the sons of Aaron, the priests, shall blow with the trumpets; and they shall be to you for an ordinance for ever throughout your generations. [9] And if ye go to _____ in your land against the enemy that oppresseth you, then ye shall blow an alarm with the trumpets; and ye shall be remembered before the Lord your God, and ye shall be _____ from your enemies. [10] Also in the day of your _____ , and in your _____ days, and in the beginnings of your months, ye shall blow with the trumpets over your burnt offerings, and over the sacrifices of your peace offerings; that they may be to you for a memorial before your God: I am the Lord your God.

[11] And it came to pass on the twentieth day of the second month, in the second year, that the cloud was taken up from off the tabernacle of the testimony. [12] And the children of Israel took their journeys out of the wilderness of Sinai; and the cloud rested in the wilderness of _____ . [13] And they first took their journey according to the commandment of the Lord by the hand of Moses.

[14] In the first place went the standard of the camp of the children of Judah according to their armies: and over his host was Nahshon the son of Amminadab. [15] And over the host of the tribe of the children of _____ was Nethaneel the son of Zuar. [16] And over the host of the tribe of the children of _____ was Eliab the son of Helon. [17] And the tabernacle was taken down; and the sons of _____ and the sons of _____ set forward, bearing the tabernacle.

[18] And the standard of the camp of _____ set forward according to their armies: and over his host was Elizur the son of Shedeur. [19] And over the host of the tribe of the children of _____ was Shelumiel the son of Zurishaddai. [20] And over the host of the tribe of the children of _____ was Eliasaph the son of Deuel. [21] And the _____ set forward, bearing the sanctuary: and the other did set up the tabernacle against they came.

[22] And the standard of the camp of the children of _____ set forward according to their armies: and over his host was Elishama the son of Ammihud. [23] And over the host of the tribe of the children of _____ was Gamaliel the son of Pedahzur. [24] And over the host of the tribe of the children of _____ was Abidan the son of Gideoni.

[25] And the standard of the camp of the children of _____ set forward, which was the rereward of all the camps throughout their hosts: and over his host was Ahiezer the son of Ammishaddai. [26] And over the host of the tribe of the children of _____ was Pagiel the son of Ocran. [27] And over the host of the tribe of the children of _____ was Ahira the son of Enan. [28] Thus were the journeyings of the children of Israel according to their armies, when they set forward.

[29] And Moses said unto Hobab, the son of Raguel the Midianite, Moses' father in law, We are journeying unto the place of which the Lord said, I will give it you: come thou with us, and we will do thee good: for the Lord hath spoken good concerning Israel. [30] And he said unto him, I will not go; but I will depart to mine own land, and to my kindred. [31] And he said, Leave us not, I pray thee; forasmuch as thou knowest how we are to encamp in the wilderness, and thou mayest be to us instead of eyes. [32] And it shall be, if thou go with us, yea, it shall be, that what goodness the Lord shall do unto us, the same will we do unto thee.

[33] And they departed from the mount of the Lord three days' journey: and the ark of the covenant of the Lord went before them in the three days' journey, to search out a resting place for them. [34] And the cloud of the Lord was upon them by day, when they went out of the camp. [35] And it came to pass, when the ark set forward, that Moses said, Rise up, Lord, and let thine enemies be scattered; and let them that hate thee flee before thee. [36] And when it rested, he said, Return, O Lord, unto the many thousands of Israel.

[11:1] And when the people _____ , it _____ the Lord: and the Lord _____ it; and his _____ was kindled; and the _____ of the Lord _____ among them, and _____ them that were in the uttermost parts of the camp. [2] And the people cried unto Moses; and when Moses prayed unto the Lord, the fire was quenched. [3] And he called the name of the place Taberah: because the fire of the Lord burnt among them.

[4] And the _____ multitude that was among them fell a _____ : and the children of Israel also _____ again, and said, Who shall give us flesh to eat? [5] We remember the fish, which we did eat in Egypt freely; the cucumbers, and the melons, and the leeks, and the onions, and the garlick: [6] But now our _____ is dried away: there is _____ at all, beside this _____ , before our eyes. [7] And the manna was as coriander seed, and the colour thereof as the colour of bdellium. [8] And the people went about, and gathered it, and ground it in mills, or beat it in a mortar, and baked it in pans, and made cakes of it: and the taste of it was as the taste of fresh _____ . [9] And when the dew fell upon the camp in the night, the manna fell upon it.

[10] Then Moses heard the people _____ throughout their families, every man in the door of his tent: and the _____ of the Lord was kindled greatly; Moses also was _____ . [11] And Moses said unto the Lord, Wherefore hast thou _____ thy servant? and wherefore have I not found favour in thy sight, that thou layest the burden of

all this people upon me? [12] Have I conceived all this people? have I begotten them, that thou shouldest say unto me, Carry them in thy bosom, as a nursing father beareth the sucking child, unto the land which thou swarest unto their fathers? [13] Whence should I have flesh to give unto all this people? for they weep unto me, saying, Give us flesh, that we may eat. [14] I am not able to bear all this people alone, because it is too heavy for me. [15] And if thou deal thus with me, kill me, I pray thee, out of hand, if I have found favour in thy sight; and let me not see my wretchedness.

[16] And the Lord said unto Moses, Gather unto me seventy men of the elders of Israel, whom thou knowest to be the elders of the people, and officers over them; and bring them unto the tabernacle of the congregation, that they may stand there with thee. [17] And I will come down and talk with thee there: and I will take of the _____ which is upon thee, and will put it upon them; and they shall _____ the burden of the people with thee, that thou bear it not thyself alone. [18] And say thou unto the people, Sanctify yourselves against to morrow, and ye shall eat flesh: for ye have wept in the ears of the Lord, saying, Who shall give us flesh to eat? for it was well with us in Egypt: therefore the Lord will give you flesh, and ye shall eat. [19] Ye shall not eat one day, nor two days, nor five days, neither ten days, nor twenty days; [20] But even a whole month, until it come out at your _____ , and it be loathsome unto you: because that ye have despised the Lord which is among you, and have wept before him, saying, Why came we forth out of Egypt? [21] And Moses said, The people, among whom I am, are six hundred thousand footmen; and thou hast said, I will give them flesh, that they may eat a whole month. [22] Shall the flocks and the herds be slain for them, to suffice them? or shall all the fish of the sea be gathered together for them, to suffice them? [23] And the Lord said unto Moses, Is the _____ hand waxed _____ ? thou shalt see now whether my _____ shall come to pass unto thee or not.

[24] And Moses went out, and told the people the words of the Lord, and gathered the seventy men of the elders of the people, and set them round about the tabernacle. [25] And the Lord came down in a cloud, and spake unto him, and took of the _____ that was upon him, and gave it unto the seventy _____ : and it came to pass, that, when the spirit rested upon them, they _____ , and did not cease. [26] But there remained two of the men in the camp, the name of the one was Eldad, and the name of the other Medad: and the _____ rested upon them; and they were of them that were written, but went not out unto the tabernacle: and they _____ in the _____ . [27] And there ran a young man, and told Moses, and said, _____ and _____ do _____ in the _____ . [28] And Joshua the son of Nun, the servant of Moses, one of his young men, answered and said, My lord Moses, _____ them. [29] And Moses said unto him, Enviest thou for my sake? would God that _____ the Lord's _____ were _____ , and that the Lord would put his _____ upon them! [30] And _____ gat him into the _____ , he and the _____ of Israel.

[31] And there went forth a _____ from the Lord, and brought _____ from the sea, and let them fall by the camp, as it were a day's journey on this side, and as it were a day's journey on the other side, round about the camp, and as it were _____ cubits high upon the face of the earth. [32] And the people _____ up all that day, and all that night, and all the next day, and they _____ the quails: he that gathered least gathered ten homers: and they spread them all abroad for themselves round about

the camp. [33] And while the flesh was yet between their teeth, ere it was chewed, the _____ of the Lord was kindled against the people, and the Lord _____ the people with a very great _____ . [34] And he called the name of that place Kibroth-hattaavah: because there they _____ the people that _____ . [35] And the people journeyed from Kibroth-hattaavah unto Hazeroth; and abode at Hazeroth.

[12:1] And Miriam and Aaron spake against Moses because of the Ethiopian woman whom he had married: for he had married an Ethiopian woman. [2] And they said, Hath the Lord indeed spoken _____ by _____ ? hath he not spoken also by _____ ? And the Lord _____ it. [3] (Now the man Moses was very _____ , above all the men which were upon the face of the earth.) [4] And the Lord spake suddenly unto Moses, and unto Aaron, and unto Miriam, Come out ye three unto the tabernacle of the congregation. And they three came out. [5] And the Lord came down in the pillar of the cloud, and stood in the door of the tabernacle, and called Aaron and Miriam: and they both came forth. [6] And he said, Hear now my words: If there be a prophet among you, I the Lord will make myself known unto him in a _____ , and will speak unto him in a _____ . [7] My servant Moses is not so, who is _____ in all mine house. [8] With him will I speak mouth to mouth, even apparently, and not in dark speeches; and the similitude of the Lord shall he behold: wherefore then were ye not _____ to speak _____ my _____ Moses? [9] And the anger of the Lord was kindled against them; and he departed. [10] And the cloud departed from off the tabernacle; and, behold, Miriam became _____ , white as snow: and Aaron looked upon Miriam, and, behold, she was leprous. [11] And Aaron said unto Moses, Alas, my lord, I beseech thee, lay not the sin upon us, wherein we have done _____ , and wherein we have sinned. [12] Let her not be as one dead, of whom the flesh is half consumed when he cometh out of his mother's womb. [13] And Moses cried unto the Lord, saying, _____ her _____ , O God, I beseech thee.

[14] And the Lord said unto Moses, If her father had but spit in her face, should she not be ashamed _____ days? let her be shut out from the camp seven days, and after that let her be received in again. [15] And Miriam was shut out from the camp seven days: and the people journeyed not till Miriam was brought in again. [16] And afterward the people removed from Hazeroth, and pitched in the wilderness of Paran.

[13:1] And the Lord spake unto Moses, saying, [2] Send thou _____ , that they may _____ the land of _____ , which I _____ unto the children of Israel: of every tribe of their fathers shall ye send a man, every one a ruler among them. [3] And Moses by the commandment of the Lord sent them from the wilderness of Paran: all those men were heads of the children of Israel. [4] And these were their names: of the tribe of Reuben, _____ the son of Zaccur. [5] Of the tribe of Simeon, _____ the son of Hori. [6] Of the tribe of Judah, _____ the son of Jephunneh. [7] Of the tribe of Issachar, _____ the son of Joseph. [8] Of the tribe of Ephraim, _____ the son of Nun. [9] Of the tribe of Benjamin, _____ the son of Raphu. [10] Of the tribe of Zebulun, _____ the son of Sodi. [11] Of the tribe of Joseph, namely, of the tribe of Manasseh, _____ the son of Susi. [12] Of the tribe of Dan, _____ the son of Gemalli. [13] Of the tribe of Asher, _____ the son of Michael. [14] Of the tribe of Naphtali, _____ the son of Vophsi. [15] Of the tribe of Gad, _____ the son of Machi. [16] These are the names of the men which Moses sent to _____ out the land. And Moses called _____ the son of Nun _____ .

[17] And Moses sent them to _____ out the land of _____ , and said unto them, Get you up this way southward, and go up into the mountain: [18] And see the land, what it is; and the people that dwelleth therein, whether they be strong or weak, few or many; [19] And what the land is that they dwell in, whether it be good or bad; and what cities they be that they dwell in, whether in tents, or in strong holds; [20] And what the land is, whether it be fat or lean, whether there be wood therein, or not. And be ye of good _____ , and bring of the _____ of the land. Now the time was the time of the firstripe _____ .

[21] So they went up, and searched the land from the wilderness of Zin unto Rehob, as men come to Hamath. [22] And they ascended by the south, and came unto Hebron; where Ahiman, Sheshai, and Talmai, the children of Anak, were. (Now Hebron was built seven years before Zoan in Egypt.) [23] And they came unto the brook of _____ , and cut down from thence a _____ with _____ cluster of _____ , and they bare it between _____ upon a staff; and they brought of the pomegranates, and of the figs. [24] The place was called the brook Eshcol, because of the cluster of grapes which the children of Israel cut down from thence. [25] And they returned from searching of the land after _____ days.

[26] And they went and came to Moses, and to Aaron, and to all the congregation of the children of Israel, unto the wilderness of Paran, to Kadesh; and brought back word unto them, and unto all the congregation, and shewed them the fruit of the land. [27] And they told him, and said, We came unto the land whither thou sentest us, and surely it floweth with _____ and _____ ; and this is the _____ of it. [28] Nevertheless the _____ be _____ that dwell in the land, and the cities are _____ , and very great: and moreover we saw the children of _____ there. [29] The _____ dwell in the land of the south: and the Hittites, and the Jebusites, and the Amorites, dwell in the mountains: and the Canaanites dwell by the sea, and by the coast of Jordan. [30] And Caleb _____ the people before Moses, and said, Let us go up at _____ , and _____ it; for we are well able to overcome it. [31] But the men that went up with him said, We be not able to go up against the people; for they are stronger than we. [32] And they brought up an _____ report of the land which they had searched unto the children of Israel, saying, The land, through which we have gone to search it, is a land that eateth up the inhabitants thereof; and all the people that we saw in it are men of a great _____ . [33] And there we saw the _____ , the sons of Anak, which come of the giants: and we were in our _____ sight as _____ , and so we were in _____ sight.

[14:1] And all the congregation lifted up their voice, and cried; and the people wept that night. [2] And all the children of Israel _____ against Moses and against Aaron: and the whole congregation said unto them, Would God that we had _____ in the land of _____ ! or would God we had _____ in this _____ ! [3] And wherefore hath the Lord brought us unto this land, to fall by the _____ , that our wives and our children should be a _____ ? were it not _____ for us to _____ into Egypt? [4] And they said one to another, Let us make a _____ , and let us _____ into Egypt. [5] Then Moses and Aaron fell on their faces before all the assembly of the congregation of the children of Israel.

[6] And _____ the son of Nun, and _____ the son of Jephunneh, which were of them that searched the land, _____ their clothes: [7] And they _____

unto all the company of the children of Israel, saying, The land, which we passed through to search it, is an exceeding _____ land. [8] If the Lord _____ in us, then he will bring us into this land, and give it us; a land which floweth with milk and honey. [9] Only _____ not ye against the _____ , neither fear ye the people of the land; for they are bread for us: their defence is departed from them, and the _____ is with us: _____ them not. [10] But all the congregation bade _____ them with stones. And the glory of the Lord appeared in the tabernacle of the congregation before all the children of Israel.

[11] And the _____ said unto Moses, How long will this people provoke me? and how long will it be ere they _____ me, for all the signs which I have shewed among them? [12] I will smite them with the _____ , and disinherit them, and will make of thee a greater nation and mightier than they.

[13] And Moses said unto the Lord, Then the Egyptians shall hear it, (for thou broughtest up this people in thy might from among them;) [14] And they will tell it to the inhabitants of this land: for they have heard that thou Lord art among this people, that thou Lord art seen face to face, and that thy cloud standeth over them, and that thou goest before them, by daytime in a pillar of a cloud, and in a pillar of fire by night.

[15] Now if thou shalt kill all this people as one man, then the nations which have heard the fame of thee will speak, saying, [16] Because the Lord was not _____ to bring this people into the land which he sware unto them, therefore he hath slain them in the wilderness. [17] And now, I beseech thee, let the power of my Lord be great, according as thou hast spoken, saying, [18] The Lord is _____ , and of great _____ , _____ iniquity and transgression, and by no means clearing the guilty, visiting the iniquity of the fathers upon the children unto the third and fourth generation. [19] _____ , I beseech thee, the iniquity of this people according unto the greatness of thy mercy, and as thou hast forgiven this people, from Egypt even until now. [20] And the Lord said, I have pardoned according to thy word: [21] But as truly as I live, all the earth shall be filled with the _____ of the Lord. [22] Because all those men which have seen my glory, and my miracles, which I did in Egypt and in the wilderness, and have tempted me now these ten times, and have not hearkened to my voice; [23] Surely they shall _____ see the land which I sware unto their fathers, neither shall any of them that provoked me see it: [24] But my servant _____ , because he had another _____ with him, and hath followed me _____ , him will I bring into the land whereinto he went; and his seed shall possess it. [25] (Now the Amalekites and the Canaanites dwelt in the valley.) To morrow turn you, and get you into the wilderness by the way of the Red sea.

[26] And the Lord spake unto Moses and unto Aaron, saying, [27] How long shall I bear with this evil congregation, which murmur against me? I have heard the murmurings of the children of Israel, which they murmur against me. [28] Say unto them, As truly as I live, saith the Lord, as ye have spoken in mine ears, so will I do to you: [29] Your carcases shall fall in this wilderness; and all that were numbered of you, according to your whole number, from _____ years old and upward, which have _____ against me, [30] Doubtless ye shall not come into the land, concerning which I sware to make you dwell therein, save _____ the son of Jephunneh, and _____ the son of Nun. [31] But your _____ ones, which ye said should be a _____ , them will I bring in, and they shall know the land which ye have despised. [32] But as for you,

your carcases, they shall fall in this wilderness. [33] And your children shall _____ in the wilderness _____ years, and bear your whoredoms, until your carcases be wasted in the wilderness. [34] After the number of the days in which ye searched the land, even forty days, each day for a year, shall ye bear your iniquities, even forty years, and ye shall know my breach of promise. [35] I the Lord have said, I will surely do it unto all this evil congregation, that are gathered together against me: in this wilderness they shall be consumed, and there they shall die. [36] And the men, which Moses sent to search the land, who returned, and made all the congregation to murmur against him, by bringing up a slander upon the land, [37] Even those _____ that did bring up the evil _____ upon the land, _____ by the _____ before the Lord. [38] But _____ the son of Nun, and _____ the son of Jephunneh, which were of the men that went to search the land, lived still. [39] And Moses told these sayings unto all the children of Israel: and the people _____ greatly.

[40] And they rose up early in the morning, and gat them up into the top of the mountain, saying, Lo, we be here, and will go up unto the place which the Lord hath promised: for we have _____ . [41] And Moses said, Wherefore now do ye transgress the commandment of the Lord? but it shall not prosper. [42] Go _____ up, for the Lord is not among you; that ye be not smitten before your enemies. [43] For the _____ and the Canaanites are there before you, and ye shall fall by the _____ : because ye are turned away from the Lord, therefore the _____ will _____ be _____ you. [44] But they _____ to go up unto the hill top: nevertheless the _____ of the covenant of the Lord, and Moses, departed not out of the camp. [45] Then the Amalekites came down, and the Canaanites which dwelt in that hill, and _____ them, and discomfited them, even unto Hormah.

[15:1] And the Lord spake unto Moses, saying, [2] Speak unto the children of Israel, and say unto them, When ye be come into the land of your habitations, which I give unto you, [3] And will make an offering by fire unto the Lord, a burnt offering, or a sacrifice in performing a vow, or in a freewill offering, or in your solemn feasts, to make a sweet savour unto the Lord, of the herd, or of the flock: [4] Then shall he that offereth his offering unto the Lord bring a meat offering of a tenth deal of flour mingled with the fourth part of an hin of _____ . [5] And the fourth part of an hin of wine for a drink offering shalt thou prepare with the burnt offering or sacrifice, for one lamb. [6] Or for a ram, thou shalt prepare for a meat offering two tenth deals of flour mingled with the third part of an hin of _____ . [7] And for a drink offering thou shalt offer the third part of an hin of wine, for a sweet savour unto the Lord. [8] And when thou preparest a bullock for a burnt offering, or for a sacrifice in performing a vow, or peace offerings unto the Lord: [9] Then shall he bring with a bullock a meat offering of three tenth deals of flour mingled with half an hin of _____ . [10] And thou shalt bring for a drink offering half an hin of wine, for an offering made by fire, of a sweet savour unto the Lord. [11] Thus shall it be done for one bullock, or for one ram, or for a lamb, or a kid. [12] According to the number that ye shall prepare, so shall ye do to every one according to their number. [13] All that are born of the country shall do these things after this manner, in offering an offering made by fire, of a sweet savour unto the Lord. [14] And if a stranger sojourn with you, or whosoever be among you in your generations, and will offer an offering made by fire, of a sweet savour unto the Lord; as ye do, so he shall do. [15] One ordinance shall be both for you of the congregation, and also for the stranger that sojourneth with you, an ordinance for ever in your generations: as ye are, so shall the stranger be before the Lord. [16] One _____ and one _____ shall be for you, and for the stranger that sojourneth with you.

[17] And the Lord spake unto Moses, saying, [18] Speak unto the children of Israel, and say unto them, When ye come into the land whither I bring you, [19] Then it shall be, that, when ye eat of the bread of the land, ye shall offer up an heave offering unto the Lord. [20] Ye shall offer up a cake of the first of your dough for an heave offering: as ye do the heave offering of the threshingfloor, so shall ye heave it. [21] Of the first of your dough ye shall give unto the Lord an heave offering in your generations.

[22] And if ye have _____ , and not observed all these commandments, which the Lord hath spoken unto Moses, [23] Even all that the Lord hath commanded you by the hand of Moses, from the day that the Lord commanded Moses, and henceforward among your generations; [24] Then it shall be, if _____ be committed by _____ without the knowledge of the congregation, that all the congregation shall offer one young bullock for a burnt offering, for a sweet savour unto the Lord, with his meat offering, and his drink offering, according to the manner, and one kid of the goats for a sin offering. [25] And the priest shall make an _____ for all the congregation of the children of Israel, and it shall be _____ them; for it is _____ : and they shall bring their offering, a sacrifice made by fire unto the Lord, and their sin offering before the Lord, for their ignorance: [26] And it shall be _____ all the congregation of the children of Israel, and the stranger that sojourneth among them; seeing all the people were in _____ .

[27] And if any soul sin through _____ , then he shall bring a she goat of the first year for a sin offering. [28] And the priest shall make an atonement for the soul that sinneth ignorantly, when he sinneth by ignorance before the Lord, to make an atonement for him; and it shall be forgiven him. [29] Ye shall have one law for him that sinneth through ignorance, both for him that is born among the children of Israel, and for the stranger that sojourneth among them.

[30] But the soul that doeth ought _____ , whether he be born in the land, or a stranger, the same reproacheth the Lord; and that soul shall be cut off from among his people. [31] Because he hath _____ the _____ of the Lord, and hath _____ his commandment, that soul shall utterly be cut off; his iniquity shall be upon him.

[32] And while the children of Israel were in the wilderness, they found a man that gathered sticks upon the _____ day. [33] And they that found him gathering sticks brought him unto Moses and Aaron, and unto all the congregation. [34] And they put him in ward, because it was not declared what should be done to him. [35] And the Lord said unto Moses, The man shall be surely put to _____ : all the congregation shall stone him with stones without the camp. [36] And all the congregation brought him without the camp, and _____ him with stones, and he died; as the Lord commanded Moses.

[37] And the Lord spake unto Moses, saying, [38] Speak unto the children of Israel, and bid them that they make them _____ in the _____ of their garments throughout their generations, and that they put upon the fringe of the borders a _____ of _____ : [39] And it shall be unto you for a _____ , that ye may _____ upon it, and _____ all the commandments of the Lord, and _____ them; and that ye seek _____ after your own heart and your own eyes,

after which ye use to go a whoring: [40] That ye may _____ , and _____ all my commandments, and be _____ unto your God. [41] I am the Lord your God, which brought you out of the land of Egypt, to be your God: I am the Lord your God.

[16:1] Now _____ , the son of Izhar, the son of Kohath, the son of Levi, and _____ and _____ , the sons of Eliab, and _____ , the son of Peleth, sons of Reuben, took men: [2] And they _____ up before _____ , with certain of the children of Israel, _____ hundred and _____ princes of the assembly, famous in the congregation, men of renown: [3] And they gathered themselves together _____ Moses and _____ Aaron, and said unto them, Ye take too _____ upon you, seeing all the congregation are _____ , every one of them, and the Lord is among them: wherefore then _____ ye up yourselves _____ the congregation of the Lord? [4] And when Moses heard it, he fell upon his face: [5] And he spake unto Korah and unto all his company, saying, Even to morrow the Lord will shew who are his, and who is holy; and will cause him to come near unto him: even him whom he hath chosen will he cause to come near unto him. [6] This do; Take you censers, Korah, and all his company; [7] And put fire therein, and put incense in them before the Lord to morrow: and it shall be that the man whom the Lord doth choose, he shall be holy: ye take too much upon you, ye sons of Levi. [8] And Moses said unto Korah, Hear, I pray you, ye sons of Levi: [9] _____ it but a _____ thing unto you, that the God of Israel hath separated you from the congregation of Israel, to bring you near to himself to do the service of the tabernacle of the Lord, and to stand before the congregation to minister unto them? [10] And he hath brought thee near to him, and all thy brethren the sons of Levi with thee: and _____ ye the _____ also? [11] For which cause both thou and all thy company are gathered together _____ the _____ : and what is _____ , that ye _____ against him?

[12] And Moses _____ to call _____ and _____ , the sons of Eliab: which said, We will _____ come up: [13] Is it a small thing that thou hast brought us up out of a land that floweth with milk and honey, to kill us in the wilderness, except thou make thyself altogether a prince over us? [14] Moreover thou hast not brought us into a land that floweth with milk and honey, or given us inheritance of fields and vineyards: wilt thou put out the eyes of these men? we will not come up. [15] And Moses was very _____ , and said unto the Lord, _____ not thou their offering: I have not taken one ass from them, neither have I _____ one of them. [16] And Moses said unto _____ , Be thou and all thy company before the Lord, thou, and they, and Aaron, to morrow: [17] And take every man his censer, and put incense in them, and bring ye before the Lord every man his censer, two hundred and fifty censers; thou also, and Aaron, each of you his censer. [18] And they took every man his censer, and put fire in them, and laid incense thereon, and stood in the door of the tabernacle of the congregation with Moses and Aaron. [19] And Korah gathered all the congregation _____ them unto the door of the tabernacle of the congregation: and the glory of the Lord appeared unto all the congregation. [20] And the Lord spake unto Moses and unto Aaron, saying, [21] _____ yourselves from among this congregation, that I may _____ them in a moment. [22] And they fell upon their faces, and said, O God, the _____ of the _____ of all _____ , shall _____ man _____ , and wilt thou be _____ with _____ the congregation?

[23] And the Lord spake unto Moses, saying, [24] Speak unto the congregation, saying, Get you up from about the tabernacle of Korah, Dathan, and Abiram. [25] And Moses rose up and went unto Dathan and Abiram; and the elders of Israel followed him. [26] And he spake unto the congregation, saying, _____ , I pray you, from the _____ of these _____ men, and touch _____ of theirs, lest ye be _____ in all their sins. [27] So they gat up from the tabernacle of Korah, Dathan, and Abiram, on every side: and Dathan and Abiram came out, and _____ in the _____ of their tents, and their _____ , and their _____ , and their _____ children. [28] And Moses said, Hereby ye shall know that the Lord hath sent me to do all these works; for I have _____ done them of mine own mind. [29] If these men _____ the _____ death of all men, or if they be _____ after the visitation of all men; then the Lord hath _____ sent me. [30] But if the Lord make a _____ thing, and the _____ open her mouth, and _____ them up, with all that appertain unto them, and they go down _____ into the _____ ; then ye shall understand that these men have _____ the Lord.

[31] And it came to pass, as he had made an end of speaking all these words, that the ground _____ asunder that was under them: [32] And the earth _____ her mouth, and _____ them up, and their houses, and all the men that appertained unto Korah, and all their _____ . [33] They, and all that appertained to them, went down _____ into the pit, and the earth _____ upon them: and they _____ from among the congregation. [34] And all Israel that were round about them fled at the cry of them: for they said, Lest the earth swallow us up also. [35] And there came out a _____ from the Lord, and consumed the _____ hundred and _____ men that offered incense.

[36] And the Lord spake unto Moses, saying, [37] Speak unto Eleazar the son of Aaron the priest, that he take up the censers out of the burning, and scatter thou the fire yonder; for they are hallowed. [38] The censers of these _____ against their own souls, let them make them broad plates for a covering of the altar: for they offered them before the Lord, therefore they are hallowed: and they shall be a sign unto the children of Israel. [39] And Eleazar the priest took the brasen censers, wherewith they that were burnt had offered; and they were made broad plates for a covering of the altar: [40] To be a memorial unto the children of Israel, that no stranger, which is not of the seed of Aaron, come near to offer incense before the Lord; that he be not as _____ , and as his _____ : as the Lord said to him by the hand of Moses.

[41] But on the _____ all the congregation of the children of Israel _____ against Moses and against Aaron, saying, Ye have _____ the people of the _____ . [42] And it came to pass, when the congregation was gathered against Moses and against Aaron, that they looked toward the tabernacle of the congregation: and, behold, the cloud covered it, and the glory of the Lord appeared. [43] And Moses and Aaron came before the tabernacle of the congregation.

[44] And the Lord spake unto Moses, saying, [45] Get you up from among this congregation, that I may consume them as in a moment. And they fell upon their faces.

[46] And Moses said unto Aaron, Take a censer, and put fire therein from off the altar, and put on incense, and go quickly unto the congregation, and make an atonement for them: for there is wrath gone out from the Lord; the _____ is begun. [47] And Aaron took as Moses commanded, and ran into the _____ of the congregation; and,

NUMBERS

behold, the _____ was begun among the people: and he put on incense, and made an _____ for the people. [48] And he stood _____ the _____ and the _____ ; and the plague was stayed. [49] Now they that died in the plague were _____ thousand and _____ hundred, beside them that died about the matter of Korah. [50] And Aaron returned unto Moses unto the door of the tabernacle of the congregation: and the plague was stayed.

[17:1] And the Lord spake unto Moses, saying, [2] Speak unto the children of Israel, and take of every one of them a _____ according to the house of their fathers, of all their princes according to the house of their fathers _____ rods: write thou every man's _____ upon his rod. [3] And thou shalt write _____ name upon the rod of Levi: for one rod shall be for the head of the house of their fathers. [4] And thou shalt lay them up in the tabernacle of the congregation before the testimony, where I will meet with you. [5] And it shall come to pass, that the man's rod, whom I shall _____ , shall _____ : and I will make to _____ from me the _____ of the children of Israel, whereby they murmur against you.

[6] And Moses spake unto the children of Israel, and every one of their princes gave him a rod apiece, for each prince one, according to their fathers' houses, even twelve rods: and the rod of Aaron was among their rods. [7] And Moses laid up the rods before the Lord in the tabernacle of witness. [8] And it came to pass, that on the morrow Moses went into the tabernacle of witness; and, behold, the _____ of _____ for the house of Levi was budded, and brought forth _____ , and bloomed _____ , and yielded _____ . [9] And Moses brought out all the rods from before the Lord unto all the children of Israel: and they looked, and took every man his rod.

[10] And the Lord said unto Moses, Bring Aaron's rod again before the testimony, to be kept for a _____ against the _____ ; and thou shalt quite take away their murmurings from me, that they die not. [11] And Moses did so: as the Lord commanded him, so did he. [12] And the children of Israel spake unto Moses, saying, Behold, we die, we perish, we all perish. [13] Whosoever cometh any thing near unto the tabernacle of the Lord shall die: shall we be consumed with dying?

[18:1] And the Lord said unto Aaron, Thou and thy sons and thy father's house with thee shall bear the iniquity of the sanctuary: and thou and thy sons with thee shall bear the iniquity of your priesthood. [2] And thy brethren also of the tribe of Levi, the tribe of thy father, bring thou with thee, that they may be joined unto thee, and minister unto thee: but thou and thy sons with thee shall minister before the tabernacle of witness. [3] And they shall keep thy charge, and the charge of all the tabernacle: only they shall not come nigh the vessels of the sanctuary and the altar, that neither they, nor ye also, die. [4] And they shall be joined unto thee, and keep the charge of the tabernacle of the congregation, for all the service of the tabernacle: and a stranger shall not come nigh unto you. [5] And ye shall keep the charge of the sanctuary, and the charge of the altar: that there be no wrath any more upon the children of Israel. [6] And I, behold, I have taken your brethren the Levites from among the children of Israel: to you they are given as a gift for the Lord, to do the service of the tabernacle of the congregation. [7] Therefore thou and thy sons with thee shall keep your priest's office for every thing of the altar, and _____ the vail; and ye shall serve: I have given your priest's office unto you as a _____ of gift: and the stranger that cometh nigh shall be put to death.

NUMBERS

[8] And the Lord spake unto Aaron, Behold, I also have given thee the charge of mine heave offerings of all the hallowed things of the children of Israel; unto thee have I given them by reason of the anointing, and to thy sons, by an ordinance for ever. [9] This shall be thine of the most holy things, reserved from the fire: every oblation of theirs, every meat offering of theirs, and every sin offering of theirs, and every trespass offering of theirs, which they shall render unto me, shall be most _____ for _____ and for thy sons. [10] In the most holy place shalt thou _____ it; every male shall _____ it: it shall be holy unto thee. [11] And this is _____ ; the _____ offering of their gift, with all the _____ offerings of the children of Israel: I have given them unto thee, and to thy sons and to thy daughters with thee, by a statute for ever: every one that is clean in thy house shall _____ of it. [12] All the _____ of the _____ , and all the _____ of the _____ , and of the _____ , the _____ of them which they shall offer unto the Lord, them have I given _____ . [13] And whatsoever is _____ ripe in the land, which they shall bring unto the Lord, shall be _____ ; every one that is clean in thine house shall _____ of it. [14] Every thing _____ in Israel shall be _____ . [15] Every thing that openeth the matrix in all flesh, which they bring unto the Lord, whether it be of men or beasts, shall be thine: nevertheless the firstborn of man shalt thou surely _____ , and the firstling of unclean beasts shalt thou _____ . [16] And those that are to be redeemed from a month old shalt thou redeem, according to thine estimation, for the _____ of five shekels, after the shekel of the sanctuary, which is twenty gerahs. [17] But the firstling of a cow, or the firstling of a sheep, or the firstling of a goat, thou shalt _____ redeem; they are holy: thou shalt sprinkle their _____ upon the altar, and shalt burn their fat for an offering made by fire, for a sweet savour unto the Lord. [18] And the _____ of them shall be _____ , as the wave _____ and as the right _____ are _____ . [19] All the heave offerings of the holy things, which the children of Israel offer unto the Lord, have I given thee, and thy sons and thy daughters with thee, by a statute for ever: it is a covenant of _____ for ever before the Lord unto thee and to thy seed with thee.

[20] And the Lord spake unto Aaron, Thou shalt have no inheritance in their land, neither shalt thou have any part among them: I am thy part and thine inheritance among the children of Israel. [21] And, behold, I have given the children of Levi all the _____ in Israel for an _____ , for their _____ which they serve, even the service of the tabernacle of the congregation. [22] Neither must the children of Israel henceforth come nigh the tabernacle of the congregation, lest they bear sin, and die. [23] But the Levites shall do the service of the tabernacle of the congregation, and they shall bear their iniquity: it shall be a statute for ever throughout your generations, that among the children of Israel they have no inheritance. [24] But the _____ of the children of Israel, which they offer as an heave offering unto the Lord, I have _____ to the _____ to _____ : therefore I have said unto them, Among the children of Israel they shall have no inheritance.

[25] And the Lord spake unto Moses, saying, [26] Thus speak unto the Levites, and say unto them, When ye take of the children of Israel the _____ which I have given you from them for your inheritance, then ye shall offer up an heave offering of it for the Lord, even a _____ part of the _____ . [27] And this your heave offering shall be reckoned unto you, as though it were the corn of the threshingfloor, and as the

28

NUMBERS

fulness of the winepress. [28] Thus ye also shall offer an heave offering unto the Lord of all your _____ , which ye receive of the children of Israel; and ye shall give thereof the Lord's heave offering to Aaron the priest. [29] Out of _____ your _____ ye shall _____ every heave offering of the Lord, of all the _____ thereof, even the _____ part thereof out of it. [30] Therefore thou shalt say unto them, When ye have _____ the _____ thereof from it, then it shall be counted unto the _____ as the _____ of the threshingfloor, and as the _____ of the winepress. [31] And ye shall eat it in every place, ye and your households: for it is _____ for your _____ in the tabernacle of the congregation. [32] And ye shall bear no sin by reason of it, when ye have heaved from it the _____ of it: neither shall ye _____ the _____ things of the children of Israel, lest ye die.

[19:1] And the Lord spake unto Moses and unto Aaron, saying, [2] This is the ordinance of the law which the Lord hath commanded, saying, Speak unto the children of Israel, that they bring thee a _____ _____ without spot, wherein is no blemish, and upon which never came yoke: [3] And ye shall give her unto Eleazar the priest, that he may bring her forth _____ the camp, and one shall slay her before his face: [4] And Eleazar the priest shall take of her _____ with his finger, and sprinkle of her blood directly before the tabernacle of the congregation seven times: [5] And one shall burn the heifer in his sight; her skin, and her flesh, and her blood, with her dung, shall he burn: [6] And the priest shall take cedar wood, and hyssop, and scarlet, and cast it into the midst of the burning of the heifer. [7] Then the priest shall wash his clothes, and he shall bathe his flesh in water, and afterward he shall come into the camp, and the priest shall be unclean until the even. [8] And he that burneth her shall wash his clothes in water, and bathe his flesh in water, and shall be unclean until the even. [9] And a _____ that is _____ shall gather up the _____ of the heifer, and _____ them _____ _____ the camp in a clean place, and it shall be kept for the congregation of the children of Israel for a water of separation: it is a purification for sin. [10] And he that gathereth the ashes of the heifer shall wash his clothes, and be unclean until the even: and it shall be unto the children of Israel, and unto the stranger that sojourneth among them, for a statute for ever.

[11] He that toucheth the dead body of any man shall be unclean seven days. [12] He shall purify himself with it on the third day, and on the seventh day he shall be clean: but if he purify not himself the third day, then the seventh day he shall not be clean. [13] Whosoever toucheth the dead body of any man that is dead, and purifieth not himself, defileth the tabernacle of the Lord; and that soul shall be cut off from Israel: because the water of separation was not sprinkled upon him, he shall be unclean; his uncleanness is yet upon him. [14] This is the law, when a man _____ in a tent: all that come into the tent, and all that is in the tent, shall be unclean seven days. [15] And every open vessel, which hath no _____ bound upon it, is unclean. [16] And whosoever toucheth one that is slain with a sword in the open fields, or a dead body, or a bone of a man, or a grave, shall be unclean seven days. [17] And for an _____ person they shall take of the _____ of the burnt heifer of _____ for sin, and running water shall be put thereto in a vessel: [18] And a clean person shall take hyssop, and dip it in the water, and sprinkle it upon the tent, and upon all the vessels, and upon the persons that were there, and upon him that touched a bone, or one slain, or one dead, or a grave: [19] And the clean person shall sprinkle upon the unclean on the third day, and on

the seventh day: and on the seventh day he shall purify himself, and wash his clothes, and bathe himself in water, and shall be clean at even. [20] But the man that shall be unclean, and shall not purify himself, that soul shall be cut off from among the congregation, because he hath defiled the sanctuary of the Lord: the water of separation hath not been sprinkled upon him; he is unclean. [21] And it shall be a perpetual statute unto them, that he that sprinkleth the water of separation shall wash his clothes; and he that toucheth the water of separation shall be unclean until even. [22] And whatsoever the unclean person toucheth shall be unclean; and the soul that toucheth it shall be unclean until even.

[20:1] Then came the children of Israel, even the whole congregation, into the desert of Zin in the first month: and the people abode in Kadesh; and _____ _____ there, and was buried there. [2] And there was no _____ for the congregation: and they _____ themselves together _____ Moses and _____ Aaron. [3] And the people _____ with Moses, and spake, saying, Would God that we had died when our _____ died before the Lord! [4] And why have ye brought up the congregation of the Lord into this wilderness, that we and our cattle should die there? [5] And wherefore have ye made us to come up out of Egypt, to bring us in unto this _____ place? it is no place of seed, or of figs, or of vines, or of pomegranates; neither is there any water to drink. [6] And Moses and Aaron went from the presence of the assembly unto the door of the tabernacle of the congregation, and they fell upon their faces: and the glory of the Lord appeared unto them.

[7] And the Lord spake unto Moses, saying, [8] Take the _____ , and gather thou the assembly together, thou, and Aaron thy brother, and _____ ye unto the _____ before their eyes; and it shall _____ forth _____ water, and thou shalt bring forth to them _____ out of the _____ : so thou shalt give the congregation and their beasts drink. [9] And Moses took the rod from before the Lord, as he commanded him. [10] And Moses and Aaron gathered the congregation together before the _____ , and he said unto them, Hear now, ye rebels; must we fetch you water out of this _____ ? [11] And Moses lifted up his hand, and with his _____ he _____ the rock _____ : and the water came out abundantly, and the congregation drank, and their beasts also.

[12] And the Lord spake unto Moses and Aaron, Because ye _____ me not, to sanctify me in the eyes of the children of Israel, therefore ye shall not bring this congregation into the land which I have given them. [13] This is the water of Meribah; because the children of Israel strove with the Lord, and he was sanctified in them.

[14] And Moses sent messengers from Kadesh unto the king of Edom, Thus saith thy brother Israel, Thou knowest all the travail that hath befallen us: [15] How our fathers went down into Egypt, and we have dwelt in Egypt a long time; and the Egyptians vexed us, and our fathers: [16] And when we cried unto the Lord, he heard our voice, and sent an _____ , and hath brought us forth out of Egypt: and, behold, we are in Kadesh, a city in the uttermost of thy border: [17] Let us pass, I pray thee, through thy country: we will not pass through the fields, or through the vineyards, neither will we drink of the water of the wells: we will go by the king's high way, we will not turn to the right hand nor to the left, until we have passed thy borders. [18] And Edom said unto him, Thou shalt not pass by me, lest I come out against thee with the sword. [19] And the children of Israel said unto him, We will go by the high way: and if I and my cattle drink of thy water, then I will pay for it: I will only, without doing any thing else, go through on my

NUMBERS

feet. [20] And he said, Thou shalt not go through. And Edom came out against him with much people, and with a strong hand. [21] Thus Edom refused to give Israel passage through his border: wherefore Israel turned away from him.

[22] And the children of Israel, even the whole congregation, journeyed from Kadesh, and came unto mount Hor. [23] And the Lord spake unto Moses and Aaron in mount Hor, by the coast of the land of Edom, saying, [24] Aaron shall be gathered unto his people: for he shall not enter into the land which I have given unto the children of Israel, because ye _____ against my _____ at the water of Meribah. [25] Take Aaron and Eleazar his son, and bring them up unto mount Hor: [26] And _____ Aaron of his garments, and put them upon Eleazar his son: and Aaron shall be gathered unto his people, and shall _____ there. [27] And Moses did as the Lord commanded: and they went up into mount Hor in the sight of all the congregation. [28] And Moses _____ Aaron of his garments, and put them upon Eleazar his son; and Aaron _____ there in the top of the mount: and Moses and Eleazar came down from the mount. [29] And when all the congregation saw that Aaron was dead, they mourned for Aaron thirty days, even all the house of Israel.

[21:1] And when king Arad the Canaanite, which dwelt in the south, heard tell that Israel came by the way of the _____ ; then he _____ against Israel, and took some of them _____ . [2] And Israel vowed a vow unto the Lord, and said, If thou wilt indeed deliver this people into my hand, then I will utterly destroy their cities. [3] And the Lord hearkened to the voice of Israel, and delivered up the Canaanites; and they utterly destroyed them and their cities: and he called the name of the place Hormah.

[4] And they journeyed from mount Hor by the way of the Red sea, to compass the land of Edom: and the soul of the people was much discouraged because of the way. [5] And the _____ spake _____ God, and _____ Moses, Wherefore have ye brought us up out of Egypt to die in the wilderness? for there is no _____ , neither is there any _____ ; and our soul _____ this light bread. [6] And the Lord sent _____ _____ among the people, and they _____ the people; and much people of Israel _____ .

[7] Therefore the people came to Moses, and said, We have _____ , for we have _____ against the _____ , and against _____ ; pray unto the Lord, that he take away the serpents from us. And Moses prayed for the people. [8] And the Lord said unto Moses, Make thee a fiery serpent, and set it upon a _____ : and it shall come to pass, that every one that is bitten, when he _____ upon it, shall _____ . [9] And Moses made a _____ of _____ , and put it upon a _____ , and it came to pass, that if a serpent had bitten any man, when he _____ the serpent of brass, he _____ .

[10] And the children of Israel set forward, and pitched in Oboth. [11] And they journeyed from Oboth, and pitched at Ije-abarim, in the wilderness which is before _____ , _____ the _____ .

[12] From thence they removed, and pitched in the valley of _____ . [13] From thence they removed, and pitched on the other side of _____ , which is in the wilderness that cometh out of the coasts of the Amorites: for Arnon is the border of Moab, between Moab and the _____ . [14] Wherefore it is said in the book of the wars of the Lord, What he did in the Red sea, and in the brooks of Arnon, [15] And at the stream of the brooks that goeth down to the dwelling of Ar, and lieth upon the border of

Moab. [16] And from thence they went to _____ : that is the well whereof the Lord spake unto Moses, Gather the people together, and I will give them _____ .

[17] Then Israel _____ this song, _____ up, O _____ ; sing ye unto it: [18] The princes _____ the _____ , the nobles of the _____ digged it, by the direction of the _____ , with their _____ . And from the wilderness they went to _____ : [19] And from Mattanah to _____ : and from Nahaliel to _____ : [20] And from Bamoth in the _____ , that is in the country of _____ , to the _____ of _____ , which looketh toward _____ .

[21] And Israel sent messengers unto _____ king of the _____ , saying, [22] Let me pass through thy land: we will not turn into the fields, or into the vineyards; we will not drink of the waters of the well: but we will go along by the king's high way, until we be past thy borders. [23] And Sihon would _____ suffer Israel to pass through his border: but Sihon gathered all his people together, and went out _____ Israel into the wilderness: and he came to Jahaz, and _____ against Israel. [24] And Israel _____ him with the edge of the sword, and _____ his land from Arnon unto Jabbok, even unto the children of Ammon: for the border of the children of Ammon was strong. [25] And Israel took all these cities: and Israel _____ in all the _____ of the Amorites, in Heshbon, and in all the _____ thereof. [26] For Heshbon was the city of Sihon the king of the Amorites, who had fought against the former king of Moab, and taken all his land out of his hand, even unto Arnon. [27] Wherefore they that speak in proverbs say, Come into Heshbon, let the city of Sihon be built and prepared: [28] For there is a fire gone out of Heshbon, a flame from the city of Sihon: it hath consumed Ar of Moab, and the lords of the high places of Arnon. [29] _____ to thee, _____ ! thou art undone, O people of Chemosh: he hath given his sons that escaped, and his daughters, into captivity unto Sihon king of the Amorites. [30] We have shot at them; Heshbon is perished even unto Dibon, and we have laid them waste even unto Nophah, which reacheth unto Medeba.

[31] Thus _____ dwelt in the land of the Amorites. [32] And Moses sent to _____ out Jaazer, and they took the _____ thereof, and _____ out the Amorites that were there.

[33] And they turned and went up by the way of Bashan: and _____ the king of Bashan went out against them, he, and all his people, to the battle at Edrei. [34] And the Lord said unto Moses, _____ him _____ : for I have _____ him into thy hand, and all his people, and his land; and thou shalt do to him as thou didst unto _____ king of the _____ , which dwelt at Heshbon. [35] So they _____ him, and his sons, and all his people, until there was none left him alive: and they _____ his land.

[22:1] And the children of Israel set forward, and pitched in the plains of Moab on this side _____ by _____ .

[2] And _____ the son of Zippor saw all that Israel had done to the Amorites. [3] And Moab was sore _____ of the people, because they were many: and Moab was distressed because of the children of Israel. [4] And Moab said unto the elders of _____ , Now shall this company lick up all that are round about us, as the ox licketh up the grass of the field. And Balak the son of Zippor was _____ of the Moabites at that time. [5] He sent messengers therefore unto _____ the son of Beor to Pethor, which is by the river of the land of the children of his people, to call him,

saying, Behold, there is a people come out from Egypt: behold, they cover the face of the earth, and they abide over against me: [6] Come now therefore, I pray thee, _____ me this _____ ; for they are too mighty for me: peradventure I shall prevail, that we may smite them, and that I may drive them out of the land: for I wot that he whom thou _____ is _____ , and he whom thou _____ is _____ . [7] And the elders of Moab and the elders of Midian departed with the _____ of divination in their hand; and they came unto _____ , and spake unto him the words of Balak. [8] And he said unto them, Lodge here this night, and I will bring you word again, as the Lord shall speak unto me: and the princes of Moab abode with Balaam. [9] And _____ came unto Balaam, and said, What men are these with thee? [10] And Balaam said unto God, Balak the son of Zippor, king of Moab, hath sent unto me, saying, [11] Behold, there is a people come out of Egypt, which covereth the face of the earth: come now, curse me them; peradventure I shall be able to overcome them, and drive them out. [12] And God said unto Balaam, Thou shalt _____ go with them; thou shalt _____ curse the people: for they are _____ . [13] And Balaam rose up in the morning, and said unto the princes of Balak, Get you into your land: for the Lord _____ to give me leave to go with you. [14] And the princes of Moab rose up, and they went unto Balak, and said, Balaam _____ to come with us.

[15] And Balak sent yet again princes, more, and more honourable than they. [16] And they came to Balaam, and said to him, Thus saith Balak the son of Zippor, Let nothing, I pray thee, hinder thee from coming unto me: [17] For I will _____ thee unto very great honour, and I will do _____ thou sayest unto me: come therefore, I pray thee, curse me this people. [18] And Balaam answered and said unto the servants of Balak, If Balak would give me his house full of _____ and _____ , I cannot go beyond the _____ of the Lord my God, to do _____ or _____ . [19] Now therefore, I pray you, tarry ye also here this night, that I may know what the Lord will say unto me more. [20] And God came unto Balaam at night, and said unto him, If the men come to call thee, _____ up, and _____ with them; but yet the _____ which _____ shall say unto thee, that shalt thou _____ . [21] And Balaam rose up in the morning, and saddled his ass, and went with the princes of Moab.

[22] And God's _____ was kindled because he _____ : and the _____ of the Lord stood in the way for an adversary against him. Now he was riding upon his _____ , and his two servants were with him. [23] And the ass saw the _____ of the Lord standing in the way, and his _____ drawn in his hand: and the ass turned aside out of the way, and went into the _____ : and Balaam _____ the ass, to turn her into the way. [24] But the angel of the Lord stood in a _____ of the _____ , a _____ being on this side, and a _____ on that side. [25] And when the ass saw the angel of the Lord, she thrust herself unto the wall, and _____ Balaam's _____ against the wall: and he _____ her again. [26] And the angel of the Lord went further, and _____ in a _____ place, where was no _____ to turn either to the _____ hand or to the _____ . [27] And when the ass _____ the angel of the Lord, she _____ down under Balaam: and Balaam's anger was kindled, and he _____ the ass with a staff. [28] And the _____ opened the _____ of the ass, and she _____ unto Balaam, What have I done unto thee, that thou hast smitten me these three times? [29] And Balaam said unto the ass, Because thou hast mocked me: I would there were a

sword in mine hand, for now would I kill thee. [30] And the ass _____ unto Balaam, Am not I thine ass, upon which thou hast ridden ever since I was thine unto this day? was I ever wont to do so unto thee? And he said, _____ . [31] Then the Lord opened the eyes of Balaam, and he saw the angel of the Lord _____ in the way, and his _____ drawn in his hand: and he _____ down his head, and fell flat on his face. [32] And the _____ of the _____ said unto him, Wherefore hast thou _____ thine ass these three times? behold, I went out to _____ thee, because thy way is _____ before me: [33] And the ass _____ me, and _____ from me these _____ times: unless she had _____ from me, surely now also I had _____ thee, and _____ her alive. [34] And Balaam said unto the _____ of the Lord, I have _____ ; for I knew not that thou stoodest in the _____ against me: now therefore, if it _____ thee, I will get me _____ again. [35] And the angel of the Lord said unto Balaam, _____ with the men: but _____ the _____ that I shall speak unto thee, that thou shalt _____ . So Balaam went with the princes of Balak.

[36] And when Balak heard that Balaam was come, he went out to meet him unto a city of Moab, which is in the border of Arnon, which is in the utmost coast. [37] And Balak said unto Balaam, Did I not earnestly send unto thee to call thee? wherefore camest thou not unto me? am I not able indeed to promote thee to honour? [38] And Balaam said unto Balak, Lo, I am come unto thee: have I now any _____ at all to say any thing? the _____ that _____ putteth in my _____ , that shall I _____ . [39] And Balaam went with Balak, and they came unto Kirjath-huzoth. [40] And Balak offered oxen and sheep, and sent to Balaam, and to the princes that were with him. [41] And it came to pass on the morrow, that Balak took Balaam, and brought him up into the _____ places of _____ , that thence he might see the utmost part of the people.

[23:1] And Balaam said unto Balak, Build me here _____ altars, and prepare me here _____ oxen and _____ rams. [2] And Balak did as Balaam had spoken; and Balak and Balaam offered on every altar a bullock and a ram. [3] And Balaam said unto Balak, Stand by thy burnt offering, and I will go: peradventure the Lord will come to meet me: and whatsoever he sheweth me I will tell thee. And he went to an high place. [4] And _____ met _____ : and he said unto him, I have prepared seven altars, and I have offered upon every altar a bullock and a ram. [5] And the Lord put a word in Balaam's mouth, and said, Return unto Balak, and thus thou shalt speak. [6] And he returned unto him, and, lo, he stood by his burnt sacrifice, he, and all the princes of Moab. [7] And he took up his parable, and said, Balak the king of Moab hath brought me from Aram, out of the mountains of the east, saying, Come, curse me Jacob, and come, defy Israel. [8] How shall I _____ , whom _____ hath _____ cursed? or how shall I _____ , whom the _____ hath not _____ ? [9] For from the top of the rocks I see him, and from the hills I behold him: lo, the people shall dwell alone, and shall not be reckoned among the nations. [10] Who can count the dust of Jacob, and the number of the fourth part of Israel? Let me die the death of the _____ , and let my last end be like his! [11] And Balak said unto Balaam, What hast thou done unto me? I took thee to _____ mine enemies, and, behold, thou hast _____ them altogether. [12] And he answered and said, Must I not take heed to speak that which the _____ hath put in my _____ ? [13] And Balak said unto him, Come, I pray thee, with me unto _____ place, from whence thou mayest see them: thou shalt see but the utmost part of them, and shalt not see them all: and _____ me them from thence.

[14] And he brought him into the field of Zophim, to the top of _____ , and built seven altars, and offered a bullock and a ram on every altar. [15] And he said unto Balak, Stand here by thy burnt offering, while I meet the Lord yonder. [16] And the Lord met Balaam, and put a word in his mouth, and said, Go again unto Balak, and say thus. [17] And when he came to him, behold, he stood by his burnt offering, and the princes of Moab with him. And Balak said unto him, What hath the Lord spoken? [18] And he took up his parable, and said, Rise up, Balak, and hear; hearken unto me, thou son of Zippor: [19] _____ is not a _____ , that he should _____ ; neither the son of man, that he should _____ : hath he _____ , and shall he not _____ it? or hath he _____ , and shall he not make it _____ ? [20] Behold, I have received commandment to _____ : and he hath _____ ; and I cannot _____ it. [21] He hath not beheld iniquity in Jacob, neither hath he seen perverseness in Israel: the Lord his God is _____ him, and the shout of a king is among them. [22] God brought them out of Egypt; he hath as it were the strength of an unicorn. [23] Surely there is no enchantment against Jacob, neither is there any divination against Israel: according to this time it shall be said of Jacob and of Israel, What hath God wrought! [24] Behold, the people shall rise up as a great lion, and lift up himself as a young lion: he shall not lie down until he eat of the prey, and drink the blood of the slain.

[25] And Balak said unto Balaam, Neither _____ them at all, nor _____ them at all. [26] But Balaam answered and said unto Balak, Told not I thee, saying, All that the Lord speaketh, that I must do?

[27] And Balak said unto Balaam, Come, I pray thee, I will bring thee unto _____ place; peradventure it will _____ God that thou mayest _____ me them from thence. [28] And Balak brought Balaam unto the top of _____ , that looketh toward Jeshimon. [29] And Balaam said unto Balak, Build me here seven altars, and prepare me here seven bullocks and seven rams. [30] And Balak did as Balaam had said, and offered a bullock and a ram on every altar.

[24:1] And when Balaam saw that it _____ the Lord to _____ Israel, he went not, as at other times, to seek for enchantments, but he set his face toward the wilderness. [2] And Balaam lifted up his eyes, and he saw Israel abiding in his tents according to their tribes; and the _____ of God came upon him. [3] And he took up his parable, and said, Balaam the son of Beor hath said, and the man whose eyes are open hath said: [4] He hath said, which heard the words of God, which saw the vision of the Almighty, falling into a trance, but having his eyes open: [5] How _____ are thy _____ , O Jacob, and thy _____ , O Israel! [6] As the _____ are they spread forth, as _____ by the river's side, as the _____ of lign aloes which the _____ hath _____ , and as _____ trees beside the _____ . [7] He shall pour the water out of his _____ , and his seed shall be in many waters, and his king shall be higher than Agag, and his kingdom shall be exalted. [8] God brought him forth out of Egypt; he hath as it were the strength of an unicorn: he shall eat up the nations his enemies, and shall break their bones, and pierce them through with his arrows. [9] He couched, he lay down as a lion, and as a great lion: who shall stir him up? _____ is he that _____ thee, and _____ is he that _____ thee.

[10] And Balak's anger was kindled against Balaam, and he _____ his hands together: and Balak said unto Balaam, I _____ thee to _____ mine enemies, and, behold, thou hast altogether _____ them these _____ times. [11] Therefore now flee thou to thy place: I thought to _____ thee unto great _____ ; but, lo, the _____ hath kept thee _____ from honour. [12] And Balaam said unto Balak, Spake I not also to thy messengers which thou sentest unto me, saying, [13] If Balak would give me his house full of silver and gold, I cannot go beyond the commandment of the Lord, to do either good or bad of mine own mind; but what the Lord saith, that will I speak? [14] And now, behold, I go unto my people: come therefore, and I will _____ thee what this people shall do to thy people in the latter days.

[15] And he took up his parable, and said, Balaam the son of Beor hath said, and the man whose eyes are open hath said: [16] He hath said, which heard the words of God, and knew the knowledge of the most High, which saw the vision of the Almighty, falling into a trance, but having his eyes open: [17] I _____ see _____ , but not now: I shall behold _____ , but not nigh: there shall come a _____ out of _____ , and a _____ shall rise out of _____ , and shall smite the corners of Moab, and destroy all the children of Sheth. [18] And Edom shall be a possession, Seir also shall be a possession for his enemies; and Israel shall do valiantly. [19] Out of _____ shall come _____ that shall have _____ , and shall destroy him that remaineth of the city.

[20] And when he looked on Amalek, he took up his parable, and said, Amalek was the first of the nations; but his latter end shall be that he perish for ever. [21] And he looked on the Kenites, and took up his parable, and said, Strong is thy dwellingplace, and thou puttest thy nest in a rock. [22] Nevertheless the Kenite shall be wasted, until Asshur shall carry thee away captive. [23] And he took up his parable, and said, Alas, _____ shall live when _____ doeth this! [24] And _____ shall come from the coast of Chittim, and shall afflict Asshur, and shall afflict Eber, and he also shall perish for ever. [25] And Balaam rose up, and went and returned to his place: and Balak also went his way.

[25:1] And Israel abode in Shittim, and the people began to _____ whoredom with the _____ of Moab. [2] And they called the _____ unto the _____ of their _____ : and the people did eat, and bowed down to their gods. [3] And Israel joined himself unto Baal-peor: and the anger of the Lord was kindled against Israel. [4] And the Lord said unto Moses, Take all the _____ of the people, and _____ them up before the Lord against the _____ , that the fierce anger of the Lord may be turned away from Israel. [5] And Moses said unto the judges of Israel, Slay ye every one his men that were joined unto Baal-peor.

[6] And, behold, one of the children of Israel came and brought unto his brethren a Midianitish woman in the sight of Moses, and in the sight of all the congregation of the children of Israel, who were _____ before the door of the tabernacle of the congregation. [7] And when Phinehas, the son of Eleazar, the son of Aaron the priest, saw it, he rose up from among the congregation, and took a _____ in his hand; [8] And he went _____ the man of Israel into the _____ , and thrust both of them _____ , the man of Israel, and the _____ through her _____ . So the _____ was stayed from the children of Israel. [9] And those that died in the plague were _____ and _____ thousand.

[10] And the Lord spake unto Moses, saying, [11] Phinehas, the son of Eleazar, the son of Aaron the priest, hath _____ my wrath away from the children of Israel, while he was _____ for my sake among them, that I consumed not the children of Israel in my jealousy. [12] Wherefore say, Behold, I give unto him my covenant of _____ : [13] And he shall have it, and his seed after him, even the covenant of an everlasting priesthood; because he was _____ for his _____ , and made an atonement for the children of Israel. [14] Now the name of the Israelite that was slain, even that was slain with the Midianitish woman, was _____ , the son of Salu, a prince of a chief house among the Simeonites. [15] And the name of the Midianitish woman that was slain was _____ , the daughter of Zur; he was head over a people, and of a chief house in Midian.

[16] And the Lord spake unto Moses, saying, [17] Vex the Midianites, and smite them: [18] For they vex you with their _____ , wherewith they have beguiled you in the matter of Peor, and in the matter of Cozbi, the daughter of a prince of Midian, their sister, which was slain in the day of the plague for Peor's sake.

[26:1] And it came to pass after the plague, that the Lord spake unto Moses and unto Eleazar the son of Aaron the priest, saying, [2] Take the sum of all the congregation of the children of Israel, from twenty years old and upward, throughout their fathers' house, all that are able to go to war in Israel. [3] And Moses and Eleazar the priest spake with them in the plains of Moab by Jordan near Jericho, saying, [4] Take the sum of the people, from twenty years old and upward; as the Lord commanded Moses and the children of Israel, which went forth out of the land of Egypt.

[5] _____ , the eldest son of Israel: the children of Reuben; Hanoch, of whom cometh the family of the Hanochites: of Pallu, the family of the Palluites: [6] Of Hezron, the family of the Hezronites: of Carmi, the family of the Carmites. [7] These are the families of the Reubenites: and they that were numbered of them were _____ and _____ thousand and _____ hundred and thirty. [8] And the sons of Pallu; Eliab. [9] And the sons of Eliab; Nemuel, and Dathan, and Abiram. This is that Dathan and Abiram, which were famous in the congregation, who strove against Moses and against Aaron in the company of Korah, when they strove against the Lord: [10] And the earth opened her mouth, and swallowed them up together with Korah, when that company died, what time the fire devoured two hundred and fifty men: and they became a sign. [11] Notwithstanding the children of Korah died not.

[12] The sons of _____ after their families: of Nemuel, the family of the Nemuelites: of Jamin, the family of the Jaminites: of Jachin, the family of the Jachinites: [13] Of Zerah, the family of the Zarhites: of Shaul, the family of the Shaulites. [14] These are the families of the Simeonites, _____ and _____ thousand and _____ hundred.

[15] The children of _____ after their families: of Zephon, the family of the Zephonites: of Haggi, the family of the Haggites: of Shuni, the family of the Shunites: [16] Of Ozni, the family of the Oznites: of Eri, the family of the Erites: [17] Of Arod, the family of the Arodites: of Areli, the family of the Arelites. [18] These are the families of the children of Gad according to those that were numbered of them, _____ thousand and _____ hundred.

[19] The sons of _____ were Er and Onan: and _____ and _____ _____ in the land of Canaan. [20] And the sons of Judah after their families were;

of Shelah, the family of the Shelanites: of Pharez, the family of the Pharzites: of Zerah, the family of the Zarhites. [21] And the sons of Pharez were; of Hezron, the family of the Hezronites: of Hamul, the family of the Hamulites. [22] These are the families of Judah according to those that were numbered of them, _____ and _____ thousand and _____ hundred.

[23] Of the sons of _____ after their families: of Tola, the family of the Tolaites: of Pua, the family of the Punites: [24] Of Jashub, the family of the Jashubites: of Shimron, the family of the Shimronites. [25] These are the families of Issachar according to those that were numbered of them, _____ and _____ thousand and _____ hundred.

[26] Of the sons of _____ after their families: of Sered, the family of the Sardites: of Elon, the family of the Elonites: of Jahleel, the family of the Jahleelites. [27] These are the families of the Zebulunites according to those that were numbered of them, _____ thousand and _____ hundred.

[28] The sons of _____ after their families were _____ and _____ . [29] Of the sons of _____ : of Machir, the family of the Machirites: and Machir begat Gilead: of Gilead come the family of the Gileadites. [30] These are the sons of Gilead: of Jeezer, the family of the Jeezerites: of Helek, the family of the Helekites: [31] And of Asriel, the family of the Asrielites: and of Shechem, the family of the Shechemites: [32] And of Shemida, the family of the Shemidaites: and of Hepher, the family of the Hepherites.

[33] And Zelophehad the son of Hepher had no sons, but daughters: and the names of the daughters of Zelophehad were Mahlah, and Noah, Hoglah, Milcah, and Tirzah. [34] These are the families of _____ , and those that were numbered of them, _____ and _____ thousand and _____ hundred.

[35] These are the sons of _____ after their families: of Shuthelah, the family of the Shuthalhites: of Becher, the family of the Bachrites: of Tahan, the family of the Tahanites. [36] And these are the sons of Shuthelah: of Eran, the family of the Eranites. [37] These are the families of the sons of Ephraim according to those that were numbered of them, _____ and _____ thousand and _____ hundred. These are the sons of _____ after their families.

[38] The sons of _____ after their families: of Bela, the family of the Belaites: of Ashbel, the family of the Ashbelites: of Ahiram, the family of the Ahiramites: [39] Of Shupham, the family of the Shuphamites: of Hupham, the family of the Huphamites. [40] And the sons of Bela were Ard and Naaman: of Ard, the family of the Ardites: and of Naaman, the family of the Naamites. [41] These are the sons of Benjamin after their families: and they that were numbered of them were _____ and _____ thousand and _____ hundred.

[42] These are the sons of _____ after their families: of Shuham, the family of the Shuhamites. These are the families of Dan after their families. [43] All the families of the Shuhamites, according to those that were numbered of them, were _____ and _____ thousand and four hundred.

[44] Of the children of _____ after their families: of Jimna, the family of the Jimnites: of Jesui, the family of the Jesuites: of Beriah, the family of the Beriites. [45] Of the sons of Beriah: of Heber, the family of the Heberites: of Malchiel, the family of the Malchielites. [46] And the name of the daughter of Asher was Sarah. [47] These are the

families of the sons of Asher according to those that were numbered of them; who were _____ and _____ thousand and _____ hundred.

[48] Of the sons of _____ after their families: of Jahzeel, the family of the Jahzeelites: of Guni, the family of the Gunites: [49] Of Jezer, the family of the Jezerites: of Shillem, the family of the Shillemites. [50] These are the families of Naphtali according to their families: and they that were numbered of them were _____ and _____ thousand and _____ hundred. [51] These were the numbered of the children of Israel, _____ hundred _____ and a _____ _____ hundred and _____ .

[52] And the Lord spake unto Moses, saying, [53] Unto these the land shall be divided for an inheritance according to the number of names. [54] To many thou shalt give the more inheritance, and to few thou shalt give the less inheritance: to every one shall his inheritance be given according to those that were numbered of him. [55] Notwithstanding the land shall be divided by lot: according to the names of the tribes of their fathers they shall inherit. [56] According to the lot shall the possession thereof be divided between many and few.

[57] And these are they that were numbered of the Levites after their families: of _____ , the family of the Gershonites: of _____ , the family of the Kohathites: of _____ , the family of the Merarites. [58] These are the families of the _____ : the family of the Libnites, the family of the Hebronites, the family of the Mahlites, the family of the Mushites, the family of the Korathites. And _____ begat _____ . [59] And the name of Amram's _____ was _____ , the daughter of _____ , whom her mother bare to Levi in _____ : and she bare unto Amram _____ and _____ , and _____ their sister. [60] And unto Aaron was born _____ , and _____ , _____ , and _____ . [61] And _____ and _____ _____ , when they offered _____ fire before the Lord. [62] And those that were numbered of them were _____ and _____ thousand, all males from a month old and upward: for they were not numbered among the children of Israel, because there was no inheritance given them among the children of Israel.

[63] These are they that were numbered by Moses and _____ the _____ , who numbered the children of Israel in the plains of Moab by Jordan near Jericho. [64] But among these there was not a man of them whom Moses and Aaron the priest numbered, when they numbered the children of Israel in the wilderness of Sinai. [65] For the Lord had said of them, They shall surely die in the wilderness. And there was not left a man of them, save _____ the son of Jephunneh, and _____ the son of Nun.

[27:1] Then came the daughters of Zelophehad, the son of Hepher, the son of Gilead, the son of Machir, the son of Manasseh, of the families of Manasseh the son of Joseph: and these are the names of his daughters; Mahlah, Noah, and Hoglah, and Milcah, and Tirzah. [2] And they stood before Moses, and before Eleazar the priest, and before the princes and all the congregation, by the door of the tabernacle of the congregation, saying, [3] Our _____ died in the wilderness, and he was not in the company of them that gathered themselves together against the Lord in the company of Korah; but died in his own _____ , and had _____ sons. [4] Why should the name of our father be done away from among his family, because he hath no son? Give unto us therefore a _____ among the brethren of our father. [5] And Moses brought their _____ before the Lord.

[6] And the Lord spake unto Moses, saying, [7] The daughters of Zelophehad speak right: thou shalt surely give them a possession of an inheritance among their father's brethren; and thou shalt cause the inheritance of their father to pass unto them. [8] And thou shalt speak unto the children of Israel, saying, If a man die, and have no son, then ye shall cause his inheritance to pass unto his _____ . [9] And if he have no daughter, then ye shall give his inheritance unto his _____ . [10] And if he have no brethren, then ye shall give his inheritance unto his _____ brethren. [11] And if his father have no brethren, then ye shall give his inheritance unto his _____ that is next to him of his family, and he shall possess it: and it shall be unto the children of Israel a statute of judgment, as the Lord commanded Moses.

[12] And the Lord said unto Moses, Get thee up into this mount Abarim, and see the land which I have given unto the children of Israel. [13] And when thou hast seen it, thou also shalt be _____ unto thy people, as Aaron thy brother was gathered. [14] For ye _____ against my commandment in the desert of Zin, in the strife of the congregation, to sanctify me at the water before their eyes: that is the water of Meribah in Kadesh in the wilderness of Zin.

[15] And Moses spake unto the Lord, saying, [16] Let the Lord, the God of the spirits of all flesh, set a man over the congregation, [17] Which may go out before them, and which may go in before them, and which may lead them out, and which may bring them in; that the congregation of the Lord be not as _____ which have no _____ .

[18] And the Lord said unto Moses, Take thee _____ the son of Nun, a man in whom is the _____ , and lay thine _____ upon him; [19] And set him before Eleazar the priest, and before all the congregation; and give him a charge in their sight. [20] And thou shalt put some of thine _____ upon him, that all the congregation of the children of Israel may be _____ . [21] And he shall stand before Eleazar the priest, who shall ask _____ for him after the judgment of Urim before the Lord: at his word shall they go out, and at his word they shall come in, both he, and all the children of Israel with him, even all the congregation. [22] And Moses did as the Lord commanded him: and he took Joshua, and set him before Eleazar the priest, and before all the congregation: [23] And he laid his hands upon him, and gave him a charge, as the Lord commanded by the hand of Moses.

[28:1] And the Lord spake unto Moses, saying, [2] Command the children of Israel, and say unto them, My offering, and my bread for my sacrifices made by fire, for a sweet savour unto me, shall ye observe to offer unto me in their due season. [3] And thou shalt say unto them, This is the offering made by fire which ye shall offer unto the Lord; two lambs of the first year without spot day by day, for a continual burnt offering. [4] The one lamb shalt thou offer in the morning, and the other lamb shalt thou offer at even; [5] And a tenth part of an ephah of flour for a meat offering, mingled with the fourth part of an hin of beaten _____ . [6] It is a continual burnt offering, which was ordained in mount Sinai for a sweet savour, a sacrifice made by fire unto the Lord. [7] And the drink offering thereof shall be the fourth part of an hin for the one lamb: in the holy place shalt thou cause the strong wine to be poured unto the Lord for a drink offering. [8] And the other lamb shalt thou offer at even: as the meat offering of the morning, and as the drink offering thereof, thou shalt offer it, a sacrifice made by fire, of a sweet savour unto the Lord.

[9] And on the _____ day two lambs of the first year without spot, and two tenth deals of flour for a meat offering, mingled with _____ , and the drink offering thereof: [10] This is the burnt offering of every sabbath, beside the continual burnt offering, and his drink offering.

[11] And in the beginnings of your months ye shall offer a burnt offering unto the Lord; two young bullocks, and one ram, seven lambs of the first year without spot; [12] And three tenth deals of flour for a meat offering, mingled with _____ , for one bullock; and two tenth deals of flour for a meat offering, mingled with _____ , for one ram; [13] And a several tenth deal of flour mingled with _____ for a meat offering unto one lamb; for a burnt offering of a sweet savour, a sacrifice made by fire unto the Lord. [14] And their drink offerings shall be half an hin of wine unto a bullock, and the third part of an hin unto a ram, and a fourth part of an hin unto a lamb: this is the burnt offering of every month throughout the months of the year. [15] And one kid of the goats for a sin offering unto the Lord shall be offered, beside the continual burnt offering, and his drink offering. [16] And in the _____ day of the _____ month is the _____ of the Lord. [17] And in the _____ day of this month is the _____ : seven days shall _____ bread be eaten. [18] In the _____ day shall be an holy _____ ; ye shall do no manner of servile work therein: [19] But ye shall offer a sacrifice made by fire for a burnt offering unto the Lord; two young bullocks, and one ram, and seven lambs of the first year: they shall be unto you without blemish: [20] And their meat offering shall be of flour mingled with _____ : three tenth deals shall ye offer for a bullock, and two tenth deals for a ram; [21] A several tenth deal shalt thou offer for every lamb, throughout the seven lambs: [22] And one goat for a sin offering, to make an _____ for you. [23] Ye shall offer these beside the burnt offering in the morning, which is for a continual burnt offering. [24] After this manner ye shall offer daily, throughout the seven days, the meat of the sacrifice made by fire, of a sweet savour unto the Lord: it shall be offered beside the continual burnt offering, and his drink offering. [25] And on the _____ day ye shall have an holy _____ ; ye shall do no servile work.

[26] Also in the day of the _____ , when ye bring a new meat offering unto the Lord, after your weeks be out, ye shall have an holy _____ ; ye shall do no servile work: [27] But ye shall offer the burnt offering for a sweet savour unto the Lord; two young bullocks, one ram, seven lambs of the first year; [28] And their meat offering of flour mingled with _____ , three tenth deals unto one bullock, two tenth deals unto one ram, [29] A several tenth deal unto one lamb, throughout the seven lambs; [30] And one kid of the goats, to make an atonement for you. [31] Ye shall offer them beside the continual burnt offering, and his meat offering, (they shall be unto you without blemish) and their drink offerings.

[29:1] And in the _____ month, on the _____ day of the month, ye shall have an holy _____ ; ye shall do no servile work: it is a day of _____ the _____ unto you. [2] And ye shall offer a burnt offering for a sweet savour unto the Lord; one young bullock, one ram, and seven lambs of the first year without blemish: [3] And their meat offering shall be of flour mingled with _____ , three tenth deals for a bullock, and two tenth deals for a ram, [4] And one tenth deal for one lamb, throughout the seven lambs: [5] And one kid of the goats for a sin offering, to make an atonement for you: [6] Beside the burnt offering of the month, and his meat offering, and the daily burnt offering, and his meat offering, and their drink offerings, according unto their manner, for a sweet savour, a sacrifice made by fire unto the Lord.

[7] And ye shall have on the _____ day of this _____ month an holy _____ ; and ye shall afflict your souls: ye shall not do any work therein: [8] But ye shall offer a burnt offering unto the Lord for a sweet savour; one young bullock, one ram, and seven lambs of the first year; they shall be unto you without blemish: [9] And their meat offering shall be of flour mingled with _____ , three tenth deals to a bullock, and two tenth deals to one ram, [10] A several tenth deal for one lamb, throughout the seven lambs: [11] One kid of the goats for a sin offering; beside the sin offering of _____ , and the continual burnt offering, and the meat offering of it, and their drink offerings.

[12] And on the _____ day of the _____ month ye shall have an holy _____ ; ye shall do no servile work, and ye shall keep a feast unto the Lord _____ days: [13] And ye shall offer a burnt offering, a sacrifice made by fire, of a sweet savour unto the Lord; thirteen young bullocks, two rams, and fourteen lambs of the first year; they shall be without blemish: [14] And their meat offering shall be of flour mingled with _____ , three tenth deals unto every bullock of the thirteen bullocks, two tenth deals to each ram of the two rams, [15] And a several tenth deal to each lamb of the fourteen lambs: [16] And one kid of the goats for a sin offering; beside the continual burnt offering, his meat offering, and his drink offering.

[17] And on the _____ day ye shall offer twelve young bullocks, two rams, fourteen lambs of the first year without spot: [18] And their meat offering and their drink offerings for the bullocks, for the rams, and for the lambs, shall be according to their number, after the manner: [19] And one kid of the goats for a sin offering; beside the continual burnt offering, and the meat offering thereof, and their drink offerings.

[20] And on the _____ day eleven bullocks, two rams, fourteen lambs of the first year without blemish; [21] And their meat offering and their drink offerings for the bullocks, for the rams, and for the lambs, shall be according to their number, after the manner: [22] And one goat for a sin offering; beside the continual burnt offering, and his meat offering, and his drink offering.

[23] And on the _____ day ten bullocks, two rams, and fourteen lambs of the first year without blemish: [24] Their meat offering and their drink offerings for the bullocks, for the rams, and for the lambs, shall be according to their number, after the manner: [25] And one kid of the goats for a sin offering; beside the continual burnt offering, his meat offering, and his drink offering.

[26] And on the _____ day nine bullocks, two rams, and fourteen lambs of the first year without spot: [27] And their meat offering and their drink offerings for the bullocks, for the rams, and for the lambs, shall be according to their number, after the manner: [28] And one goat for a sin offering; beside the continual burnt offering, and his meat offering, and his drink offering.

[29] And on the _____ day eight bullocks, two rams, and fourteen lambs of the first year without blemish: [30] And their meat offering and their drink offerings for the bullocks, for the rams, and for the lambs, shall be according to their number, after the

manner: [31] And one goat for a sin offering; beside the continual burnt offering, his meat offering, and his drink offering.

[32] And on the _____ day seven bullocks, two rams, and fourteen lambs of the first year without blemish: [33] And their meat offering and their drink offerings for the bullocks, for the rams, and for the lambs, shall be according to their number, after the manner: [34] And one goat for a sin offering; beside the continual burnt offering, his meat offering, and his drink offering.

[35] On the _____ day ye shall have a _____ assembly: ye shall do no servile work therein: [36] But ye shall offer a burnt offering, a sacrifice made by fire, of a sweet savour unto the Lord: one bullock, one ram, seven lambs of the first year without blemish: [37] Their meat offering and their drink offerings for the bullock, for the ram, and for the lambs, shall be according to their number, after the manner: [38] And one goat for a sin offering; beside the continual burnt offering, and his meat offering, and his drink offering. [39] These things ye shall do unto the Lord in your set feasts, beside your vows, and your freewill offerings, for your burnt offerings, and for your meat offerings, and for your drink offerings, and for your peace offerings. [40] And Moses told the children of Israel according to all that the Lord commanded Moses.

[30:1] And Moses spake unto the _____ of the tribes concerning the children of Israel, saying, This is the thing which the Lord hath commanded. [2] If a man vow a vow unto the Lord, or swear an oath to bind his soul with a bond; he shall not _____ his _____ , he shall _____ according to all that proceedeth out of his mouth. [3] If a _____ also vow a vow unto the Lord, and bind herself by a bond, being _____ her _____ house in her _____ ; [4] And her _____ hear her vow, and her _____ wherewith she hath bound her soul, and her father shall _____ his peace at her: then all her vows shall _____ , and every bond wherewith she hath bound her soul shall stand. [5] But if her father _____ her in the _____ that he heareth; not any of her _____ , or of her _____ wherewith she hath bound her soul, shall _____ : and the Lord shall _____ her, because her father _____ her. [6] And if she had at all an _____ , when she _____ , or uttered ought out of her lips, wherewith she bound her soul; [7] And her husband heard it, and held his peace at her in the day that he heard it: then her vows shall _____ , and her bonds wherewith she bound her soul shall _____ . [8] But if her _____ _____ her on the _____ that he heard it; then he shall make her _____ which she vowed, and that which she uttered with her lips, wherewith she bound her soul, of _____ effect: and the Lord shall _____ her. [9] But every vow of a _____ , and of her that is _____ , wherewith they have bound their souls, shall _____ against her. [10] And if she vowed in her husband's _____ , or bound her soul by a bond with an oath; [11] And her _____ heard it, and held his _____ at her, and _____ her _____ : then all her vows shall _____ , and every bond wherewith she bound her soul shall stand. [12] But if her _____ hath utterly made them _____ on the _____ he heard them; then whatsoever proceeded out of her lips concerning her vows, or concerning the bond of her soul, shall _____ stand: her husband hath made them void; and the Lord shall _____ her. [13] Every vow, and every binding oath to afflict the soul, her husband may _____ it, or her husband may make it _____ . [14] But if her husband altogether hold his peace at her from _____ to day; then he _____ all her vows, or all her bonds, which are upon her: he _____ them, because he held his peace at her in the day that he heard them. [15] But if he shall any ways make them _____ after that he hath heard them; then he shall bear her iniquity. [16] These are the _____ , which the Lord commanded Moses, between a man and his wife, between the father and his daughter, being yet in her youth in her father's house.

[31:1] And the Lord spake unto Moses, saying, [2] _____ the children of Israel of the Midianites: afterward shalt thou be gathered unto thy people. [3] And Moses spake unto the people, saying, _____ some of yourselves unto the _____ , and let them go against the Midianites, and avenge the Lord of Midian. [4] Of every tribe a _____ , throughout all the tribes of Israel, shall ye send to the _____ . [5] So there were delivered out of the thousands of Israel, a thousand of every tribe, _____ thousand armed for war. [6] And Moses sent them to the _____ , a thousand of every tribe, them and _____ the son of Eleazar the priest, to the war, with the holy instruments, and the trumpets to blow in his hand. [7] And they warred against the Midianites, as the Lord commanded Moses; and they slew all the males. [8] And they slew the kings of Midian, beside the rest of them that were slain; namely, Evi, and Rekem, and Zur, and Hur, and Reba, five kings of Midian: Balaam also the son of Beor they slew with the sword. [9] And the children of Israel took all the _____ of Midian _____ , and their little ones, and took the _____ of all their cattle, and all their flocks, and all their goods. [10] And they burnt all their cities wherein they dwelt, and all their goodly castles, with fire. [11] And they took all the _____ , and all the prey, both of men and of beasts. [12] And they brought the _____ , and the prey, and the _____ _____ , unto Moses, and Eleazar the priest, and unto the congregation of the children of Israel, unto the camp at the plains of Moab, which are by Jordan near Jericho.

[13] And _____ , and _____ the priest, and all the _____ of the congregation, _____ forth to _____ them without the _____ . [14] And Moses was _____ with the _____ of the host, with the captains over thousands, and captains over hundreds, which came from the battle. [15] And Moses said unto them, Have ye _____ all the _____ alive? [16] Behold, these caused the children of Israel, through the counsel of Balaam, to commit trespass against the Lord in the matter of Peor, and there was a plague among the congregation of the Lord. [17] Now therefore _____ every male among the little ones, and kill every _____ that hath known man by lying with him. [18] But all the _____ children, that have not known a man by lying with him, keep _____ for yourselves. [19] And do ye abide without the camp seven days: whosoever hath killed any person, and whosoever hath touched any slain, purify both yourselves and your captives on the third day, and on the seventh day. [20] And purify all your raiment, and all that is made of skins, and all work of goats' hair, and all things made of wood.

[21] And Eleazar the priest said unto the men of war which went to the battle, This is the ordinance of the law which the Lord commanded Moses; [22] Only the _____ , and the _____ , the _____ , the _____ , the _____ , and the _____ , [23] Every _____ that may _____ the _____ , ye shall make it go through the fire, and it shall be _____ : nevertheless it shall be purified with the water of separation: and all that abideth not the fire ye shall make go through the

water. [24] And ye shall wash your clothes on the seventh day, and ye shall be clean, and afterward ye shall come into the camp.

[25] And the Lord spake unto Moses, saying, [26] Take the sum of the prey that was taken, both of man and of beast, thou, and Eleazar the priest, and the chief fathers of the congregation: [27] And divide the prey into two parts; between them that took the war upon them, who _____ out to battle, and between all the _____ : [28] And levy a _____ unto the Lord of the men of war which went out to battle: one soul of five hundred, both of the persons, and of the beeves, and of the asses, and of the sheep: [29] Take it of their half, and give it unto Eleazar the priest, for an heave offering of the Lord. [30] And of the children of Israel's half, thou shalt take one portion of fifty, of the persons, of the beeves, of the asses, and of the flocks, of all manner of beasts, and give them unto the Levites, which keep the charge of the tabernacle of the Lord. [31] And _____ and _____ the priest _____ as the _____ commanded Moses. [32] And the booty, being the rest of the prey which the men of war had caught, was six hundred thousand and seventy thousand and five thousand sheep, [33] And threescore and twelve thousand beeves, [34] And threescore and one thousand asses, [35] And thirty and two thousand persons in all, of women that had not known man by lying with him. [36] And the half, which was the portion of them that went out to war, was in number three hundred thousand and seven and thirty thousand and five hundred sheep: [37] And the Lord's tribute of the sheep was six hundred and threescore and fifteen. [38] And the beeves were thirty and six thousand; of which the Lord's tribute was threescore and twelve. [39] And the asses were thirty thousand and five hundred; of which the Lord's tribute was threescore and one. [40] And the persons were sixteen thousand; of which the Lord's tribute was thirty and two persons. [41] And Moses gave the _____ , which was the _____ heave offering, unto _____ the priest, as the Lord commanded Moses. [42] And of the children of Israel's half, which Moses divided from the men that warred, [43] (Now the half that pertained unto the congregation was three hundred thousand and thirty thousand and seven thousand and five hundred sheep, [44] And thirty and six thousand beeves, [45] And thirty thousand asses and five hundred, [46] And sixteen thousand persons;) [47] Even of the children of Israel's half, Moses took one portion of fifty, both of man and of beast, and gave them unto the Levites, which kept the charge of the tabernacle of the Lord; as the Lord commanded Moses.

[48] And the officers which were over thousands of the host, the captains of thousands, and captains of hundreds, came near unto Moses: [49] And they said unto Moses, Thy servants have taken the sum of the men of war which are under our charge, and there lacketh not one man of us. [50] We have therefore brought an _____ for the Lord, what every man hath gotten, of jewels of gold, chains, and bracelets, rings, earrings, and tablets, to make an _____ for our souls before the Lord. [51] And Moses and Eleazar the priest took the gold of them, even all wrought jewels. [52] And all the gold of the offering that they offered up to the Lord, of the captains of thousands, and of the captains of hundreds, was sixteen thousand seven hundred and fifty shekels. [53] (For the men of war had taken _____ , every man for himself.) [54] And Moses and Eleazar the priest took the gold of the captains of thousands and of hundreds, and brought it into the tabernacle of the congregation, for a _____ for the children of Israel before the Lord.

[32:1] Now the children of Reuben and the children of Gad had a very great multitude of cattle: and when they saw the land of Jazer, and the land of Gilead, that, behold, the place was a _____ for cattle; [2] The children of Gad and the children of Reuben came and spake unto Moses, and to Eleazar the priest, and unto the princes of the congregation, saying, [3] Ataroth, and Dibon, and Jazer, and Nimrah, and Heshbon, and Elealeh, and Shebam, and Nebo, and Beon, [4] Even the country which the Lord smote before the congregation of Israel, is a land for cattle, and thy servants have cattle: [5] Wherefore, said they, if we have found _____ in thy sight, let this land be given unto thy servants for a _____ , and bring us not over Jordan.

[6] And Moses said unto the children of Gad and to the children of Reuben, Shall your brethren go to war, and shall ye sit here? [7] And wherefore _____ ye the heart of the children of Israel from going over into the land which the Lord hath given them? [8] Thus did your fathers, when I sent them from Kadesh-barnea to see the land. [9] For when they went up unto the valley of Eshcol, and saw the land, they discouraged the heart of the children of Israel, that they should not go into the land which the Lord had given them. [10] And the Lord's _____ was kindled the same time, and he sware, saying, [11] Surely none of the men that came up out of Egypt, from twenty years old and upward, shall see the land which I sware unto Abraham, unto Isaac, and unto Jacob; because they have not wholly followed me: [12] Save Caleb the son of Jephunneh the Kenezite, and Joshua the son of Nun: for they have _____ followed the Lord. [13] And the Lord's anger was kindled against Israel, and he made them _____ in the wilderness _____ years, until all the generation, that had done evil in the sight of the Lord, was consumed. [14] And, behold, ye are risen up in your fathers' stead, an increase of sinful men, to augment yet the fierce anger of the Lord toward Israel. [15] For if ye turn _____ from after him, he will yet again leave them in the wilderness; and ye shall destroy all this people.

[16] And they came near unto him, and said, We will build sheepfolds here for our cattle, and cities for our little ones: [17] But we ourselves will _____ ready armed before the children of Israel, until we have brought them unto their place: and our little ones shall dwell in the fenced cities because of the inhabitants of the land. [18] We will not return unto our houses, until the children of Israel have inherited every man his inheritance. [19] For we will not inherit with them on _____ side _____ , or _____ ; because our inheritance is fallen to us on _____ side Jordan eastward.

[20] And Moses said unto them, If ye will _____ this thing, if ye will go armed before the Lord to war, [21] And will go all of you armed over Jordan before the Lord, until he hath driven out his enemies from before him, [22] And the land be subdued before the Lord: then afterward ye shall return, and be _____ before the Lord, and before Israel; and this land shall be your possession before the Lord. [23] But if ye will not do so, behold, ye have _____ against the Lord: and be _____ your _____ will _____ you out. [24] Build you cities for your little ones, and folds for your sheep; and do that which hath proceeded out of your mouth. [25] And the children of Gad and the children of Reuben spake unto Moses, saying, Thy servants will do as my lord commandeth. [26] Our little ones, our wives, our flocks, and all our cattle, shall be there in the cities of Gilead: [27] But thy servants will pass over, every man armed for war, before the Lord to battle, as my lord saith. [28] So concerning them

NUMBERS

Moses commanded Eleazar the priest, and Joshua the son of Nun, and the chief fathers of the tribes of the children of Israel: [29] And Moses said unto them, If the children of Gad and the children of Reuben will pass with you over Jordan, every man armed to battle, before the Lord, and the land shall be subdued before you; then ye shall give them the land of Gilead for a possession: [30] But if they will _____ pass over with you armed, they shall have possessions among you in the land of Canaan. [31] And the children of Gad and the children of Reuben answered, saying, As the Lord hath said unto thy servants, so will we do. [32] We will pass over armed before the Lord into the land of Canaan, that the possession of our inheritance on _____ side Jordan may be ours. [33] And Moses gave unto them, even to the children of _____ , and to the children of _____ , and unto _____ the tribe of _____ the son of Joseph, the kingdom of Sihon king of the Amorites, and the kingdom of Og king of Bashan, the land, with the cities thereof in the coasts, even the cities of the country round about.

[34] And the children of Gad built Dibon, and Ataroth, and Aroer, [35] And Atroth, Shophan, and Jaazer, and Jogbehah, [36] And Beth-nimrah, and Beth-haran, fenced cities: and folds for sheep. [37] And the children of Reuben built Heshbon, and Elealeh, and Kirjathaim, [38] And Nebo, and Baal-meon, (their names being changed,) and Shibmah: and gave other names unto the cities which they builded. [39] And the children of Machir the son of Manasseh went to Gilead, and took it, and dispossessed the Amorite which was in it. [40] And Moses gave Gilead unto Machir the son of Manasseh; and he dwelt therein. [41] And Jair the son of Manasseh went and took the small towns thereof, and called them Havoth-jair. [42] And Nobah went and took Kenath, and the villages thereof, and called it Nobah, after his own name.

[33:1] These are the journeys of the children of Israel, which went forth out of the land of Egypt with their armies under the hand of Moses and Aaron. [2] And Moses _____ their goings out according to their journeys by the commandment of the Lord: and these are their journeys according to their goings out. [3] And they departed from _____ in the _____ month, on the _____ day of the first month; on the _____ after the _____ the children of Israel went out with an _____ hand in the _____ of all the Egyptians. [4] For the _____ buried all their _____ , which the Lord had smitten among them: upon their _____ also the Lord executed _____ . [5] And the children of Israel _____ from Rameses, and pitched in _____ . [6] And they departed from Succoth, and pitched in _____ , which is in the edge of the wilderness. [7] And they removed from Etham, and turned again unto _____ - _____ , which is before Baal-zephon: and they pitched before _____ . [8] And they departed from before Pi-hahiroth, and passed through the midst of the _____ into the wilderness, and went _____ days' journey in the wilderness of _____ , and pitched in _____ . [9] And they removed from Marah, and came unto _____ : and in Elim were _____ fountains of _____ , and threescore and ten palm trees; and they pitched there. [10] And they removed from Elim, and encamped by the _____ sea. [11] And they removed from the Red sea, and encamped in the wilderness of _____ . [12] And they took their journey out of the wilderness of Sin, and encamped in _____ . [13] And they departed from Dophkah, and encamped in _____ . [14] And they removed from Alush, and encamped at _____ , where was _____ water for the people to _____ . [15] And they departed from Rephidim, and pitched in the wilderness of _____ . [16] And they removed from the desert of Sinai, and pitched at _____ - _____ . [17] And they departed from Kibroth-hattaavah, and encamped at _____ . [18] And they departed from Hazeroth, and pitched in _____ . [19] And they departed from Rithmah, and pitched at _____ - _____ . [20] And they departed from Rimmon-parez, and pitched in _____ . [21] And they removed from Libnah, and pitched at _____ . [22] And they journeyed from Rissah, and pitched in _____ . [23] And they went from Kehelathah, and pitched in mount _____ . [24] And they removed from mount Shapher, and encamped in _____ . [25] And they removed from Haradah, and pitched in _____ . [26] And they removed from Makheloth, and encamped at _____ . [27] And they departed from Tahath, and pitched at _____ . [28] And they removed from Tarah, and pitched in _____ . [29] And they went from Mithcah, and pitched in _____ . [30] And they departed from Hashmonah, and encamped at _____ . [31] And they departed from Moseroth, and pitched in _____ - _____ . [32] And they removed from Bene-jaakan, and encamped at _____ - _____ . [33] And they went from Hor-hagidgad, and pitched in _____ . [34] And they removed from Jotbathah, and encamped at _____ . [35] And they departed from Ebronah, and encamped at _____ - _____ . [36] And they removed from Ezion-gaber, and pitched in the wilderness of _____ , which is _____ . [37] And they removed from Kadesh, and pitched in mount _____ , in the edge of the land of _____ . [38] And _____ the priest went up into mount Hor at the commandment of the Lord, and _____ there, in the _____ year after the children of Israel were come out of the land of Egypt, in the _____ day of the _____ month. [39] And Aaron was an _____ and _____ and _____ years old when he died in mount Hor. [40] And king Arad the Canaanite, which dwelt in the south in the land of Canaan, heard of the coming of the children of Israel. [41] And they departed from mount Hor, and pitched in _____ . [42] And they departed from Zalmonah, and pitched in _____ . [43] And they departed from Punon, and pitched in _____ . [44] And they departed from Oboth, and pitched in _____ - _____ , in the border of _____ . [45] And they departed from _____ , and pitched in _____ - _____ . [46] And they removed from Dibon-gad, and encamped in _____ - _____ . [47] And they removed from Almon-diblathaim, and pitched in the mountains of _____ , before _____ . [48] And they _____ from the _____ of Abarim, and _____ in the _____ of Moab by _____ near _____ . [49] And they pitched by Jordan, from _____ - _____ even unto _____ - _____ in the plains of Moab.

   [50] And the Lord spake unto Moses in the plains of Moab by Jordan near Jericho, saying, [51] Speak unto the children of Israel, and say unto them, When ye are passed _____ Jordan _____ the land of Canaan; [52] Then ye shall _____ out _____ the inhabitants of the land from before you, and _____ all their _____ , and _____ all their _____ images, and quite _____ down all their high _____ : [53] And ye shall dispossess the inhabitants of the land, and dwell therein: for I have given you the land to possess it. [54] And ye shall divide the land by lot for an inheritance among your families: and to the more ye shall give the more inheritance, and to the fewer ye shall give the less inheritance: every man's inheritance

NUMBERS

shall be in the place where his lot falleth; according to the tribes of your fathers ye shall inherit. [55] But if ye will _____ drive _____ the inhabitants of the land from before you; then it shall come to pass, that those which ye let _____ of them shall be _____ in your _____ , and _____ in your _____ , and shall _____ you in the land wherein ye dwell. [56] Moreover it shall come to pass, that I shall _____ unto you, as I _____ to do unto them.

[34:1] And the Lord spake unto Moses, saying, [2] Command the children of Israel, and say unto them, When ye come into the land of Canaan; (this is the land that shall fall unto you for an inheritance, even the land of Canaan with the coasts thereof:) [3] Then your _____ quarter shall be from the wilderness of _____ along by the _____ of _____ , and your _____ border shall be the outmost coast of the _____ sea eastward: [4] And your border shall turn from the south to the ascent of _____ , and pass on to Zin: and the going forth thereof shall be from the south to _____ - _____ , and shall go on to _____ - _____ , and pass on to _____ : [5] And the _____ shall fetch a compass from _____ unto the _____ of Egypt, and the goings out of it shall be at the _____ . [6] And as for the western border, ye shall even have the _____ sea for a _____ : this shall be your _____ border. [7] And this shall be your _____ border: from the _____ sea ye shall point out for you mount _____ : [8] From mount Hor ye shall point out your _____ unto the entrance of _____ ; and the goings forth of the border shall be to _____ :

[9] And the _____ shall go on to _____ , and the goings out of it shall be at _____ - _____ : this shall be your _____ border. [10] And ye shall point out your _____ border from _____ - _____ to _____ : [11] And the _____ shall go down from _____ to _____ , on the _____ side of _____ ; and the border shall descend, and shall reach unto the side of the sea of _____ eastward: [12] And the _____ shall go down to _____ , and the goings out of it shall be at the _____ sea: this shall be _____ _____ with the coasts thereof round about. [13] And Moses commanded the children of Israel, saying, This is the land which ye shall inherit by lot, which the Lord commanded to give unto the _____ tribes, and to the _____ tribe: [14] For the tribe of the children of _____ according to the house of their fathers, and the tribe of the children of _____ according to the house of their fathers, have _____ their inheritance; and _____ the tribe of _____ have received their _____ : [15] The two tribes and the half tribe have received their inheritance on this side Jordan near Jericho eastward, toward the sunrising. [16] And the Lord spake unto Moses, saying, [17] These are the names of the men which shall divide the land unto you: _____ the priest, and _____ the son of Nun. [18] And ye shall take one prince of every tribe, to divide the land by inheritance. [19] And the names of the men are these: Of the tribe of Judah, Caleb the son of Jephunneh. [20] And of the tribe of the children of Simeon, Shemuel the son of Ammihud. [21] Of the tribe of Benjamin, Elidad the son of Chislon. [22] And the prince of the tribe of the children of Dan, Bukki the son of Jogli. [23] The prince of the children of Joseph, for the tribe of the children of Manasseh, Hanniel the son of Ephod. [24] And the prince of the tribe of the children of Ephraim, Kemuel the son of Shiphtan. [25] And the prince of the tribe of the children of Zebulun, Elizaphan the son of Parnach. [26] And the prince of the

tribe of the children of Issachar, Paltiel the son of Azzan. [27] And the prince of the tribe of the children of Asher, Ahihud the son of Shelomi. [28] And the prince of the tribe of the children of Naphtali, Pedahel the son of Ammihud. [29] These are they whom the Lord commanded to divide the inheritance unto the children of Israel in the land of Canaan.

[35:1] And the Lord spake unto Moses in the plains of Moab by Jordan near Jericho, saying, [2] _____ the children of Israel, that they _____ unto the _____ of the _____ of their possession cities to dwell in; and ye shall give also unto the Levites suburbs for the cities round about them. [3] And the cities shall they have to dwell in; and the suburbs of them shall be for their cattle, and for their goods, and for all their beasts. [4] And the suburbs of the cities, which ye shall give unto the Levites, shall reach from the wall of the city and outward a thousand cubits round about. [5] And ye shall measure from without the city on the _____ side _____ thousand cubits, and on the _____ side _____ thousand cubits, and on the _____ side _____ thousand cubits, and on the _____ side _____ thousand cubits and the _____ shall be in the midst: this shall be to them the suburbs of the cities. [6] And among the cities which ye shall give unto the Levites there shall be _____ cities for _____ , which ye shall appoint for the _____ , that he may _____ thither: and to them ye shall add _____ and _____ cities. [7] So all the cities which ye shall give to the Levites shall be _____ and _____ cities: them shall ye give with their suburbs. [8] And the cities which ye shall give shall be of the possession of the children of Israel: from them that have many ye shall give many; but from them that have few ye shall give few: every one shall give of his cities unto the Levites according to his inheritance which he inheriteth.

[9] And the Lord spake unto Moses, saying, [10] Speak unto the children of Israel, and say unto them, When ye be come over Jordan into the land of Canaan; [11] Then ye shall appoint you cities to be _____ of _____ for _____ ; that the _____ may _____ thither, which _____ any person at _____ . [12] And they shall be unto you cities for _____ from the _____ ; that the manslayer die not, until he _____ before the congregation in _____ . [13] And of these cities which ye shall give _____ cities shall ye have for refuge. [14] Ye shall give _____ cities on this side Jordan, and _____ cities shall ye give in the land of Canaan, which shall be cities of refuge. [15] These _____ cities shall be a _____ , both for the children of Israel, and for the stranger, and for the sojourner among them: that every one that _____ any person _____ may flee thither. [16] And if he smite him with an instrument of iron, so that he die, he is a _____ : the murderer shall surely be put to _____ . [17] And if he smite him with _____ a _____ , wherewith he may die, and he die, he is a _____ : the murderer shall surely be put to death. [18] Or if he smite him with an hand _____ of wood, wherewith he may die, and he die, he is a _____ : the murderer shall surely be put to _____ . [19] The _____ of _____ himself shall _____ the murderer: when he _____ him, he shall _____ him. [20] But if he _____ him of _____ , or _____ at him by _____ of wait, that he die; [21] Or in _____ smite him with his _____ , that he die: he that smote him shall surely be put to _____ ; for he is a _____ : the _____ of blood shall slay the murderer, when he _____ him. [22] But if

he _____ him suddenly _____ enmity, or have _____ upon him any _____ without _____ of wait, [23] Or with any _____ , wherewith a man may die, _____ him _____ , and _____ it upon him, that he _____ , and was not his _____ , neither _____ his harm: [24] Then the congregation shall _____ between the _____ and the _____ of blood according to these _____ : [25] And the congregation shall deliver the slayer out of the hand of the revenger of blood, and the congregation shall _____ him to the city of his _____ , whither he was _____ : and he shall _____ in it unto the _____ of the high _____ , which was _____ with the holy _____ . [26] But if the _____ shall at any time come _____ the border of the city of his refuge, whither he was fled; [27] And the _____ of blood find him without the borders of the city of his refuge, and the _____ of blood _____ the slayer; he shall not be _____ of blood: [28] Because he should have _____ in the city of his refuge until the death of the high priest: but after the _____ of the high priest the slayer shall return into the land of his _____ . [29] So these things shall be for a statute of judgment unto you throughout your generations in all your dwellings. [30] Whoso _____ any person, the _____ shall be put to _____ by the _____ of _____ : but _____ witness shall _____ testify against any person to cause him to _____ . [31] Moreover ye shall take no _____ for the _____ of a _____ , which is guilty of death: but he shall be surely put to _____ . [32] And ye shall take no _____ for him that is fled to the city of his refuge, that he should come again to _____ in the land, until the _____ of the priest. [33] So ye shall not _____ the land wherein ye are: for _____ it defileth the land: and the land cannot be cleansed of the blood that is shed therein, but by the blood of him that shed it. [34] Defile not therefore the land which ye shall inhabit, wherein I dwell: for I the Lord dwell among the children of Israel.

[36:1] And the chief fathers of the families of the children of Gilead, the son of Machir, the son of Manasseh, of the families of the sons of Joseph, came near, and spake before Moses, and before the princes, the chief fathers of the children of Israel: [2] And they said, The Lord commanded my lord to give the land for an inheritance by lot to the children of Israel: and my lord was commanded by the Lord to give the inheritance of Zelophehad our brother unto his daughters. [3] And if they be married to any of the sons of the other tribes of the children of Israel, then shall their inheritance be taken from the inheritance of our fathers, and shall be put to the inheritance of the tribe whereunto they are received: so shall it be taken from the lot of our inheritance. [4] And when the _____ of the children of Israel shall be, then shall their inheritance be put unto the inheritance of the tribe whereunto they are received: so shall their inheritance be taken away from the inheritance of the tribe of our fathers. [5] And Moses commanded the children of Israel according to the word of the Lord, saying, The tribe of the sons of Joseph hath said well. [6] This is the thing which the Lord doth command concerning the daughters of Zelophehad, saying, Let them _____ to whom they think best; _____ to the _____ of the _____ of their _____ shall they _____ . [7] So shall not the inheritance of the children of Israel remove from tribe to tribe: for every one of the children of Israel shall keep himself to the inheritance of the tribe of his fathers. [8] And every daughter, that possesseth an inheritance in any tribe of the children of Israel, shall be wife unto one of the family of the tribe of her father, that

the children of Israel may _____ every man the _____ of his fathers. [9]
Neither shall the inheritance _____ from one tribe to another tribe; but every one of
the tribes of the children of Israel shall keep himself to his own inheritance. [10] Even as
the Lord commanded Moses, so did the daughters of Zelophehad: [11] For Mahlah,
Tirzah, and Hoglah, and Milcah, and Noah, the daughters of Zelophehad, were married
unto their father's brothers' sons: [12] And they were married into the families of the sons
of Manasseh the son of Joseph, and their inheritance remained in the tribe of the family
of their father. [13] These are the _____ and the _____ , which the
_____ commanded by the hand of _____ unto the children of _____ in
the plains of _____ by _____ near _____ .

Made in the USA
Columbia, SC
19 June 2025

59577135R00030